The Ligl

Charles Neville Buck

Alpha Editions

This edition published in 2022

ISBN : 9789356892354

Design and Setting By
Alpha Editions
www.alphaedis.com
Email - info@alphaedis.com

Contents

CHAPTER I

AN OMEN IS CONSTRUED

"When a feller an' a gal washes their hands in the same basin at the same time, it's a tol'able good sign they won't git married this year."

The oracle spoke through the bearded lips of a farmer perched on the top step of his cabin porch. The while he construed omens, a setter pup industriously gnawed at his boot-heels.

The girl was bending forward, her fingers spread in a tin basin, as the man at her elbow poured water slowly from a gourd-dipper. Heaped, in disorder against the cabin wall, lay their red hunting-coats, crops, and riding gauntlets.

The oracle tumbled the puppy down the steps and watched its return to the attack. Then with something of melancholy retrospect in his pale eyes he pursued his reflections. "Now there was Sissy Belmire an' Bud Thomas, been keeping company for two years, then washed hands in common at the Christian Endeavor picnic an'—" He broke off to shake his head in sorrowing memory.

The young man, holding his muddied digits over the water, paused to consider the matter.

Suddenly his hands went down into the basin with a splash.

"It is now the end of October," he enlightened; "next year comes in nine weeks."

The sun was dipping into a cloud-bank already purpled and gold-rimmed. Shortly it would drop behind the bristling summit-line of the hills.

The girl looked down at tell-tale streaks of red clay on the skirt of her riding habit, and shook her head. "'Twill never, never do to go back like this," she sighed. "They'll know I've come a cropper, and they fancy I'm as breakable as Sévres. There will be no end of questions."

The young man dropped to his knees and began industriously plying a brush on the damaged skirt. The farmer took his eyes from the puppy for an upward glance. His face was solicitous.

"When I saw that horse of yours fall down, it looked to me like he was trying to jam you through to China. You sure lit hard!"

"It didn't hurt me," she laughed as she thrust her arms into the sleeves of her pink coat. "You see, we thought we knew the run better than the whips, and we chose the short cut across your meadow. My horse took off too wide at that stone fence. That's why he went down, and why we turned your house into a port of repairs. You have been very kind."

The trio started down the grass-grown pathway to the gate where the hunters stood hitched. The young man dropped back a few paces to satisfy himself that she was not concealing some hurt. He knew her half-masculine contempt for acknowledging the fragility of her sex.

Reassurance came as he watched her walking ahead with the unconscious grace that belonged to her pliant litheness and expressed itself in her superb, almost boyish carriage.

When they had mounted and he had reined his bay down to the side of her roan, he sat studying her through half-closed, satisfied eyes though he already knew her as the Moslem priest knows the Koran. While they rode in silence he conned the inventory. Slim uprightness like the strength of a young poplar; eyes that played the whole color-gamut between violet and slate-gray, as does the Mediterranean under sun and cloud-bank; lips that in repose hinted at melancholy and that broke into magic with a smile. Then there was the suggestion of a thought-furrow between the brows and a chin delicately chiseled, but resolute and fascinatingly uptilted.

It was a face that triumphed over mere prettiness with hints of challenging qualities; with individuality, with possibilities of purpose, with glints of merry humor and unspoken sadness; with deep-sleeping potentiality for passion; with a hundred charming whimsicalities.

The eyes were just now fixed on the burning beauty of the sunset and the thought-furrow was delicately accentuated. She drew a long, deep breath and, letting the reins drop, stretched out both arms toward the splendor of the sky-line.

"It is so beautiful—so beautiful!" she cried, with the rapture of a child, "and it all spells Freedom. I should like to be the freest thing that has life under heaven. What is the freest thing in the world?"

She turned her face on him with the question, and her eyes widened after a way they had until they seemed to be searching far out in the fields of untalked-of things, and seeing there something that clouded them with disquietude.

"I should like to be a man," she went on, "a man and a *hobo*." The furrow vanished and the eyes suddenly went dancing. "That is what I should like to be—a hobo with a tomato-can and a fire beside the railroad-track."

The man said nothing, and she looked up to encounter a steady gaze from eyes somewhat puzzled.

His pupils held a note of pained seriousness, and her voice became responsively vibrant as she leaned forward with answering gravity in her own.

"What is it?" she questioned. "You are troubled."

He looked away beyond her to the pine-topped hills, which seemed to be marching with lances and ragged pennants, against the orange field of the sky. Then his glance came again to her face.

"They call me the Shadow," he said slowly. "You know whose shadow that means. These weeks have made us comrades, and I am jealous because you are the sum of two girls, and I know only one of them. I am jealous of the other girl at home in Europe. I am jealous that I don't know why you, who are seemingly subject only to your own fancy, should crave the freedom of the hobo by the railroad track."

She bent forward to adjust a twisted martingale, and for a moment her face was averted. In her hidden eyes at that moment, there was deep suffering, but when she straightened up she was smiling.

"There is nothing that you shall not know. But not yet—not yet! After all, perhaps it's only that in another incarnation I was a vagrant bee and I'm homesick for its irresponsibility."

"At all events"—he spoke with an access of boyish enthusiasm—"I 'thank whatever gods may be' that I have known you as I have. I'm glad that we have not just been idly rich together. Why, Cara, do you remember the day we lost our way in the far woods, and I foraged corn, and you scrambled stolen eggs? We were forest folk that day; primitive as in the years when things were young and the best families kept house in caves."

The girl nodded. "I approve of my shadow," she affirmed.

The smile of enthusiasm died on his face and something like a scowl came there.

"The chief trouble," he said, "is that altogether too decent brute, Pagratide. I don't like double shadows; they usually stand for confused lights."

"Are you jealous of Pagratide?" she laughed. "He pretends to have a similar sentiment for you."

"Well," he conceded, laughing in spite of himself, "it does seem that when a European girl deigns to play a while with her American cousins, Europe might stay on its own side of the pond. This Pagratide is a commuter over the Northern Ocean track. He harasses the Atlantic with his goings and comings."

"The Atlantic?" she echoed mockingly.

"Possibly I was too modest," he amended. "I mean me and the Atlantic—particularly me."

From around the curve of the road sounded a tempered shout. The girl laughed.

"You seem to have summoned him out of space," she suggested.

The man growled. "The local from Europe appears to have arrived." He gathered in his reins with an almost vicious jerk which brought the bay's head up with a snort of remonstrance.

A horseman appeared at the turn of the road. Waving his hat, he put spurs to his mount and came forward at a gallop. The newcomer rode with military uprightness, softened by the informal ease of the polo-player. Even at the distance, which his horse was lessening under the insistent pressure of his heels, one could note a boyish charm in the frankness of his smile and an eagerness in his eyes.

"I have been searching for you for centuries at least," he shouted, with a pleasantly foreign accent, which was rather a nicety than a fault of enunciation, "but the quest is amply rewarded!"

He wheeled his horse to the left with a precision that again bespoke the cavalryman, and bending over the girl's gauntleted hand, kissed her fingers in a manner that added to something of ceremonious flourish much more of individual homage. Her smile of greeting was cordial, but a degree short of enthusiasm.

"I thought—" she hesitated. "I thought you were on the other side."

The newcomer's laugh showed a glistening line of the whitest teeth under a closely-cropped dark mustache.

"I have run away," he declared. "My honored father is, of course, furious, but Europe was desolate—and so—" He shrugged his shoulders. Then, noting Benton's half-amused, half-annoyed smile, he bowed and saluted. "Ah, Benton," he said. "How are you? I see that your eyes resent foreign invasion."

Benton raised his brows in simulated astonishment. "Are you still foreign?" he inquired. "I thought perhaps you had taken out your first citizenship papers."

"But you?" Pagratide turned to the girl with something of entreaty. "Will you not give me your welcome?"

In the distance loomed the tile roofs and tall chimneys of "Idle Times." Between stretched a level sweep of road.

"You didn't ask permission," she replied, with a touch of disquiet in her pupils. "When a woman is asked to extend a welcome, she must be given time to prepare it. I ran away from Europe, you know, and after all you are a part of Europe."

She shook out her reins, bending forward over the roan's neck, and with a clatter of gravel under their twelve hoofs, the horses burst forward in a sudden neck and neck dash, toward the patch of red roofs set in a mosaic of Autumn woods.

CHAPTER II

BENTON PLAYS MAGICIAN

In the large living-room, Van Bristow, the master of "Idle Times," had expressed his tastes. Here in the almost severe wainscoting, in inglenook and chimney-corner, one found the index to his fancy. It was his fancy which had dictated that the broad windows, with sills at the level of the floor, should not command the formal terraces and lawns of a landscape-gardener's devising, but should give exit instead upon a strip of rugged nature, where the murmur of the creek came up through unaltered foliage and underbrush.

Shortening their entrance through one of the windows, the trio found their host, already in evening dress. Bristow was idling on the hearth with no more immediate concern than a cigarette and the enjoyment of the crackling logs, unspoiled by other light.

As the clatter of boots and spurs announced their coming, Van glanced up and schooled his face into a very fair counterfeit of severity.

"Lucky we don't make our people ring in on the clock," he observed. "You three would be docked."

The girl stood in the red glow of the hearth, slowly drawing off her riding-gauntlets.

Pagratide went to the table in search of cigarettes and matches, and as the light there was dim, the host joined him and laid a hand readily enough upon the brass case for which the other was fumbling. As he held a light to his guest's cigarette, he bent over and spoke in a guarded undertone. Benton noticed in the brief flare that the visitor's face mirrored sudden surprise.

"Colonel Von Ritz is here," confided Bristow. "Arrived by the next train after you and was for posting off in search of you instanter. He acted very much like a summons-server or a bailiff. He's ensconced in rooms adjoining yours. You might look in on him as you go up to dress. He seems to be in the very devil of a hurry."

Pagratide's brows went up in evident annoyance and for an instant there was a defiant stiffening of his jaw, but when he spoke his voice held neither excitement nor surprise.

"Ah, indeed!" The exclamation was casual. He watched the glowing end of his cigarette for a moment, then magnanimously added: "However, since he has followed across three thousand miles, I had better see him."

The host turned to the girl. "I'm borrowing this young man until dinner," he vouchsafed as he led Pagratide to the door.

Cara stood watching the two as they passed into the hall; then her face changed suddenly as though she had been leaving a stage and had laid aside a part—abandoning a semblance which it was no longer necessary to maintain. A pained droop came to the corners of her lips and she dropped wearily into the broad oak seat of the inglenook. There she sat, with her chin propped on her hands, elbows on her knees, and gazed silently at the logs.

"Why did they have to come just now and spoil my holiday?"

She spoke as though unconscious that her musings were finding voice, and the half-whispered words were wistful. Benton took a step nearer and bent impulsively forward.

"What is it?" he anxiously questioned.

She only looked intently into the coals with trouble-clouded eyes and shook her head. He could not tell whether in response to his words or to some thought of her own.

Dropping on one knee at her feet, he gently covered her hands with his own. He could feel the delicate play of her breath on his forehead.

"Cara," he whispered, "what is it, dear?"

She started, and with a spasmodic movement caught one of his hands, for an instant pressing it in her own, then, rising, she shook her head with a gesture of the fingers at the temples as though she would brush away cobwebs that enmeshed and fogged the brain.

"Nothing, boy." Her smile was somewhat wistful. "Nothing but silly imaginings." She laughed and when she spoke again her voice was as light as if her world held only triviality and laughter. "Yet there be important things to decide. What shall I wear for dinner?"

"It's such a hard question," he demurred. "I like you best in so many things, but the queen can do no wrong—make no mistake."

A sudden shadow of pain crossed her eyes, and she caught her lower lip sharply between her teeth.

"Was it something I said?" he demanded.

"Nothing," she answered slowly. "Only don't say that again, ever—'the queen can do no wrong.' Now, I must go."

She rose and turned toward the door, then suddenly carrying one hand to her eyes, she took a single unsteady step and swayed as though she would fall. Instantly his arms were around her and for a moment he could feel, in its wild fluttering, her heart against the red breast of his hunting-coat.

Her laugh was a little shaken as she drew away from him and stood, still a trifle unsteady. Her voice was surcharged with self-contempt.

"Sir Gray Eyes, I—I ask you to believe that I don't habitually fall about into people's arms. I'm developing nerves—there is a white feather in my moral and mental plumage."

He looked at her with grave eyes, from which he sternly banished all questioning—and remained silent.

They passed out into the hall and, at the foot of the stairs where their ways diverged, she paused to look back at him with an unclouded smile.

"You have not told me what to wear."

His eyes were as steady as her own. "You will please wear the black gown with the shimmery things all over it. I can't describe it, but I can remember it. And a single red rose," he judiciously added.

"'Tis October and the florists are fifty miles away," she demurred. "It would take a magician's wand to produce the red rose."

"I noticed a funny looking thing among my golf sticks," he remembered. "It is a little bit like a niblick, but it may be a magic wand in disguise. You wear the black gown and trust to providence for the red rose."

She threw back a laugh and was gone.

When she disappeared at the turning, he wheeled and went to the "bachelors' barracks," as the master of "Idle Times" dubbed the wing where the unmarried men were quartered.

Two suites next adjoining the room allotted to Benton had been unoccupied when he had gone out that forenoon. Between his quarters and these erstwhile vacant ones lay a room forming a sort of buffer space. Here a sideboard, a card-table, and desk made the "neutral zone," as Van called it, available for his guests as a territory either separating or connecting their individual chambers.

Now a blaze of transoms and a sound of voices proclaimed that the apartments were tenanted. Benton entered his own unlighted room, and then with his hand at the electric switch halted in embarrassment.

The folding-doors between his apartment and the "neutral territory" stood wide, and the attitudes and voices of the two men he saw there indicated their interview to be one in which outsiders should have no concern. To switch on the light would be to declare himself a witness to a part at least; to remain would be to become unwilling auditor to more; to open the door he had just closed behind him would also be to attract attention to himself. He paused in momentary uncertainty.

One of the men was Pagratide, transformed by anger; seemingly taller, darker, lither. The second man stood calm, immobile, with his arms crossed on his breast, bending an impassive glance on the other from singularly steady eyes. His six feet of well-proportioned stature just missed an exaggeration of soldierly bearing.

The unwavering mouth-line; level, dark brows almost meeting over unflinching gray eyes; the uncurved nose and commanding forehead were in concert with the clean, almost lean sweep of the jaw, in spelling force for field or council.

"Am I a brigand, Von Ritz, to be harassed by police? Answer me—am I?" Pagratide spoke in a tempest of anger. He halted before the other man, his hands twitching in fury.

Von Ritz remained as motionless, apparently as mildly interested, as though he were listening to the screaming of a parrot.

"My orders were explicit." His words fell icily. "They were the orders of His Majesty's government. I shall obey them. I beg pardon, I shall attempt to obey them; and thus far my attempts to serve His Majesty have not encountered failure. I should prefer not having to call on the ambassador—or the American secret service."

"By God! If I had a sword—" breathed Pagratide. His fury had gone through heat to cold, and his attitude was that of a man denied the opportunity of resenting a mortal affront.

Von Ritz coolly inclined his head, indicating the heaped-up luggage on the table between them. Otherwise he did not move.

"The stick there, on the table, is a sword-cane," he commented.

Pagratide stood unmoving.

The other waited a moment, almost deferentially, then went on with calm deliberation.

"You left your regiment without leave, captain. One might almost call that—" Then Benton remembered an auxiliary door at the back of his apartment and made his escape unnoticed.

A half hour later, changed from boots and breeches into evening dress, Benton was opening a long package which bore the name of his florist in town. In another moment he had spread a profusion of roses on his table and stood bending over them with the critically selective gaze of a Paris.

When he had made the choice of one, he carefully pared every thorn from its long stem. Then he went out through the rear of the hall to a stairway at the back.

He knew of a window-seat above, where he could wait in concealment behind a screening mass of potted palms to rise out of his ambush and intercept Cara as she came into the hall. It pleased him to regard himself as a genie, materializing out of emptiness to present the rose which she had chosen to declare unobtainable.

In the shadowed recess he ensconced himself with his knees drawn up and the flower twirling idly between his fingers.

For a while he measured his vigil only by the ticking of a clock somewhere out of sight, then he heard a quiet footfall on the hardwood, and through the fronds of the plants he saw a man's figure pace slowly by. The broad shoulders and the lancelike carriage proclaimed Von Ritz even before the downcast face was raised. At Cara's door the European wheeled uncertainly and paused. Because something vague and subconscious in Benton's mind had catalogued this man as a harbinger of trouble and branded him with distrust, his own eyes contracted and the rose ceased twirling.

Just then the door of Cara's room opened and closed, and the slender figure of the girl stood out in the silhouette of her black evening gown against the white woodwork. Her eyes widened and she paled perceptibly. For an instant, she caught her lower lip between her teeth; but she did not, by start or other overt manifestation, give sign of surprise. She only inclined her head in greeting, and waited for Von Ritz to speak.

He bowed low, and his manner was ceremonious.

"You do not like me—" He smiled, pausing as though in doubt as to what form of address he should employ; then he asked: "What shall I call you?"

"Miss Carstow," she prompted, in a voice that seemed to raise a quarantine flag above him.

"Certainly, Miss Carstow," he continued gravely. "Time has elapsed since the days of your pinafores and braids, when I was honored with the sobriquet of 'Soldier-man' and you were the 'Little Empress.'"

His voice was one that would have lent itself to eloquence. Now its even modulation carried a sort of cold charm.

"You do not like me," he repeated.

"I don't know," she answered simply. "I hadn't thought about it. I was surprised."

"Naturally." He contemplated her with grave eyes that seemed to admit no play of expression. "I came only to ask an interview later. At any time that may be most agreeable—Pardon me," he interrupted himself with a certain cynical humor in his voice, "at any time, I should say, that may be least disagreeable to you."

"I will tell you later," she said. He bowed himself backward, then turning on his heel went silently down the stairs.

She stood hesitant for a moment, with both hands pressed against the door at her back, and her brow drawn in a deep furrow, then she threw her chin upward and shook her head with that resolute gesture which meant, with her, shaking off at least the outward seeming of annoyance.

Benton came out from his hiding-place behind the palms, and she looked up at him with a momentary clearing of her brow.

"Where were you?" she asked.

"I unintentionally played eavesdropper," he said humbly, handing her the rose. "I was lying in wait to decorate you."

"It is wonderful," she exclaimed. "I think it is the wonderfulest rose that any little girl ever had for a magic gift." She held it for a moment, softly against her cheek.

He bent forward. "Cara!" he whispered. No answer. "Cara!" he repeated.

"Yeth, thir," she lisped in a whimsical little-girl voice, looking up with a smile stolen from a fairy-tale.

"I am just lending you that rose. I had meant to give it to you, but *now* I want it back—when you are through with it. May I have it?"

She held it out teasingly. "Do you want it now—Indian-giver?" she demanded.

"You know I don't," in an injured tone.

"I'm glad, because you couldn't have it—yet." And she was gone, leaving him to make his appearance from the direction of his own apartments.

CHAPTER III

THE MOON OVERHEARS

At dinner the talk ran for a course or two with the hounds, then strayed aimlessly into a dozen discursive channels.

"My boy," whispered Mrs. Van from her end of the table, to Pagratide on her right, "I relinquish you to the girl on your other side. You have made a very brave effort to talk to me. Ah, I know—" raising a slender hand to still his polite remonstrance—"there is no Cara but Cara, and Pagratide is—" She let her mischief-laden smile finish the comment.

"Her satellite," he confessed.

"One of them," she wickedly corrected him.

The foreigner turned his head and nodded gravely. Cara was listening to something that Benton was saying in undertone, her lips parted in an amused smile.

Through a momentary lull as the coffee came, rose the voice of O'Barreton, the bore, near the head of the table; O'Barreton, who must be tolerated because as a master of hounds he had no superior and a bare quorum of equals.

"For my part," he was saying, "I confess an augmented admiration for Van because he's distantly related to near-royalty. If that be snobbish, make the most of it."

Van laughed. "Related to royalty?" he scornfully repeated. "Am I not myself a sovereign with the right on election day to stand in line behind my chauffeur and stable-boys at the voting-place?"

"How did it happen, Van? How did you acquire your gorgeous relatives?" persisted O'Barreton.

"Some day I'll tell you all about it. Do you think the Elkridge hounds will run—"

"I addressed a question to you. That question is still before the house," interrupted O'Barreton, with dignity. "How did you acquire 'em?"

"Inherited 'em!" snapped Van, but O'Barreton was not to be turned aside.

"Quite true and quite epigrammatic," he persisted sweetly. "But how?"

Van turned to the rest of the table. "You don't have to listen to this," he said in despair. "I have to go through it with O'Barreton every time he comes here. It's a sort of ritual." Then, turning to the tormenting guest, he explained carefully: "Once upon a time the Earl of Dundredge had three daughters. The eldest—my mother—married an American husband. The second married an Englishman—she is the mother of my fair cousin, Cara, there; the third and youngest married the third son of the Grand Duke of Maritzburg, at that time a quiet gentleman who loved the Champs Elysées and landscape-painting in Southern Spain."

Van traced a family-tree on the tablecloth with a salt-spoon, for his guest's better information.

"That doesn't enlighten me on the semi-royal status of your Aunt Maritzburg," objected O'Barreton. "How did she grow so great?"

"Vicissitudes, Barry," explained the host patiently. "Just vicissitudes. The father and the two elder brothers died off and left the third son to assume the government of a grand duchy, which he did not want, and compelled him to relinquish the mahl-stick and brushes which he loved. My aunt was his grand-duchess-consort, and until her death occupied with him the ducal throne. If you'd look these things up for yourself, my son, in some European 'Who's Who,' you'd remember 'em—and save me much trouble."

After dinner Cara disappeared, and Benton wandered from room to room with a seemingly purposeless eye, keenly alert for a black gown, a red rose, and a girl whom he could not find. Von Ritz also was missing, and this fact added to his anxiety.

In the conservatory he came upon Pagratide, likewise stalking about with restlessly roving eyes, like a hunter searching a jungle. The foreigner paused with one foot tapping the marble rim of a small fountain, and Benton passed with a nod.

The evening went by without her reappearance, and finally the house darkened, and settled into quiet. Benton sought the open, driven by a restlessness that obsessed and troubled him. A fitful breeze brought down the dead leaves in swirling eddies. The moon was under a cloud-bank when, a quarter of a mile from the house, he left the smooth lawns and plunged among the vine-clad trees and thickets that rimmed the creek. In the darkness, he could hear the low, wild plaint with which the stream tossed itself over the rocks that cumbered its bed.

Beyond the thicket he came again to a more open space among the trees, free from underbrush, but strewn at intervals with great bowlders. He picked his way cautiously, mindful of crevices where a broken leg or worse might be the penalty of a misstep in the darkness. The humor seized him to sit on a great rock which dropped down twenty feet to the creek bed, and listen to the quieting music of its night song. His eyes, grown somewhat accustomed to the darkness, had been blinded again by the match he had just struck to light a cigarette, and he walked, as it behooved him, carefully and gropingly.

"Please, sir, don't step on me."

Benton halted with a start and stared confusedly about him. A ripple of low laughter came to his ears as he widened his pupils in the effort to accommodate his eyes to the murk. Then the moon broke out once more and the place became one of silver light and dark, soft shadow-blots. She was sitting with her back against a tree, her knees gathered between her arms, fingers interlocked. She had thrown a long, rough cape about her, but it had fallen open, leaving visible the black gown and a spot he knew to be a red rose on her breast.

He stood looking down, and she smiled up.

"Cara!" he exclaimed. "What are you doing here—alone?"

"Seeking freedom," she responded calmly. "It's not so good as the hobo's fire beside the track, but it's better than four walls. The moon has been wonderful, Sir Gray Eyes—as bright and dark as life; radiant a little while and hidden behind clouds a great deal. And the wind has been whispering like a troubadour to the tree-tops."

"And you," he interrupted severely, dropping on the earth at her feet and propping himself on one elbow, "have been sitting in the chilling air, with your throat uncovered and probably catching cold."

"What a matter-of-fact person it is!" she laughed. "I didn't appoint you my physician, you know."

"PLEASE, SIR, DON'T STEP ON ME."

"But your coming alone out here in these woods, and so late!" he expostulated.

"Why not?" She looked frankly up at him. "I am not afraid."

"I am afraid for you." He spoke seriously.

"Why?" she inquired again.

He knelt beside her, looking directly into her eyes. "For many reasons," he said. "But above all else, because I love you."

The fingers of her clasped hands tightened until they strained, and she looked straight away across the clearing. The moon was bright now, and the thought-furrow showed deep between her brows, but she said nothing.

The tree-tops whispered, and the girl shivered slightly. He bent forward and folded the cape across her throat. Still she did not move.

"Cara, I love you," he repeated insistently.

"Don't—I can't listen." Her voice was one of forced calm. Then, turning suddenly, she laid her hand on his arm. It trembled violently under her touch. "And, oh, boy," she broke out, with a voice of pent-up vibrance, "don't you see how I want to listen to you?"

He bent forward until he was very close, and his tone was almost fierce in its tense eagerness.

"You want to! Why?"

Again a tremor seized her, then with the sudden abandon of one who surrenders to an impulse stronger than one's self, she leaned forward and placed a hand on each of his shoulders, clutching him almost wildly. Her eyes glowed close to his own.

"Because I love you, too," she said. Then, with a break in her voice: "Oh, you knew that! Why did you make me say it?"

While the stars seemed to break out in a chorus above him, he found his arms about her, and was vaguely conscious that his lips were smothering some words her lips were trying to shape. Words seemed to him just then so superfluous.

There was a tumult of pounding pulses in his veins, responsive to the fluttering heart which beat back of a crushed rose in the lithe being he held in his arms. Then he obeyed the pressure of the hands on his shoulders and released her.

"Why should you find it so hard to say?" He asked.

She sat for a moment with her hands covering her face.

"You must never do that again," she said faintly. "You have not the right. I have not the right."

"I have the only right," he announced triumphantly.

She shook her head. "Not when the girl is engaged."

She looked at him with a sad droop at the corners of her lips. He sat silent—waiting.

"Listen!" She spoke wearily, rising and leaning against the rough bole of the tree at her back, with both hands tightly clasped behind her. "Listen and don't interrupt, because it's hard, and I want to finish it." Her words came slowly with labored calm, almost as if she were reciting memorized lines. "It sounds simple from your point of view. It is simple from mine, but desperately hard. Love is not the only thing. To some of us there is something else that must come first. I am engaged, and I shall marry the man to whom I am engaged. Not because I want to, but because—" her chin went up with the determination that was in her—"because I must."

"What kind of man will ask you to keep a promise that your heart repudiates?" he hotly demanded.

"He knew that I loved you before you knew it," she answered; "that I would always love you—that I would never love him. Besides, he must do it. After all, it's fortunate that he wants to." She tried to laugh.

"Is his name Pagratide?" The man mechanically drew his handkerchief from his cuff, and wiped beads of cold moisture from his forehead.

The girl shook her head. "No, his name is not Pagratide."

He took a step nearer, but she raised a hand to wave him back, and he bowed his submission.

"You love me—you are certain of that?" he whispered.

"Do you doubt it?"

"No," he said, "I don't doubt it."

Again he pressed the handkerchief to his forehead, and in the silvering radiance of the moonlight she could see the outstanding tracery of the arteries on his temples.

Instantly she flung both arms about his neck.

"Don't!" she cried passionately. "Don't look like that! You will kill me!"

He smiled. "Under such treatment, I shall look precisely as you say," he acquiesced.

"Listen, dear." She was talking rapidly, wildly, her arms still about his neck. "There are two miserable little kingdoms over there.... Horrible little two-by-four principalities, that fit into the map of Europe like little, ragged chips in a mosaic.... Cousin Van lied in there to protect my disguise.... It is my father who is the Grand Duke of Maritzburg, and it is ordained that I shall marry Prince Karyl of Galavia.... It was Von Ritz's mission to remind me of my slavery." Her voice rose in sudden protest. "Every peasant girl in the vineyards may select her own lover, but I must be awarded by the crowned heads of the real kingdoms—like a prize in a lottery. Do you wonder that I have run away and masqueraded for a taste of freedom before the end? Do you wonder"—the head came down on his shoulder—"that I want to be a hobo with a tomato-can and a fire of deadwood?"

He kissed her hair. "Are you crying, Cara, dear?" he asked softly.

Her head came up. "I never cry," she answered. "Do you believe there are more lives—other incarnations—that I may yet live to be a butterfly—or a vagrant bee?"

"I believe"—his voice was firm—"I believe you are not Queen of Galavia yet by a good bit. There's a fairly husky American anarchist in this game, dearest, who has designs on that dynasty."

"Don't!" she begged. "Don't you see that I wouldn't let them force me? It is that I see the inexorable call of it, as my father saw it when he left his studio in Paris for a throne that meant only unhappiness—as you would see it, if your country called for volunteers."

He bowed his head. For a moment neither spoke. Then she took the rose from her breast and kissed it.

"Sir Knight of the Red Rose," she said, with a pitifully forced smile. "I don't want to give it back—ever. I want to keep it always."

He took her in his arms, and she offered no protest.

"To-morrow is to-morrow," he said. "To-day you are mine. I love you."

She took his head between her palms and drew his face down. "I shall never do this with anyone else," she said slowly, kissing his forehead. "I love you."

Slowly they turned together toward the house.

"I like your cavalryman, Pagratide," he said thoughtfully. His mind had suddenly recurred to the scene in the foreigner's room, and he thought he began to understand. "He is a man. He dares to challenge royal wrath by venturing his love in the lists against his prince."

"I wish he had not come," she said slowly.

"But you don't love him?" he demanded with sudden unreasoning jealousy.

"I love—just, only, solely, you, Mr. Monopoly," she replied.

At the door they paused. There was complete silence save for a clock striking two and the distant crowing of a cock. The pause belonged to them—their moment of reprieve.

At last she said quietly: "But you are stupid not to guess it."

"Guess what?" he inquired.

"There is no Pagratide. Pagratide's real name is Karyl of Galavia."

CHAPTER IV

THE DOCTRINE ACCORDING TO JONESY

If the living-room at "Idle Times" bore the impress of Van Bristow's individuality and taste, his den was the tangible setting of his personality.

His marriage had, only eighteen months before, cut his life sharply with the boundary of an epoch. The den bore something of the atmosphere of a museum dedicated to past eras. It was crowded with useless junk that stood for divers memories and much wandering. Many of the pictures that cumbered the walls were redolent of the atmosphere of overseas.

There were photographs wherein the master of "Idle Times" and Mr. George Benton appeared together, ranging from ancient football days to snapshots of a mountain-climbing expedition in the Andes, dated only two years back.

It was into this sanctum that Benton clanked, booted and spurred, early the following morning.

Ostensibly Van was looking over business letters, but there was a trace of wander-lust in the eyes that strayed off with dreamy truancy beyond the tree-tops.

Benton planted himself before his host with folded arms, and stood looking down almost accusingly into the face of his old friend.

"Whenever I have anything particularly unpleasant to do," began the guest, "I do it quick. That's why I'm here now."

Van Bristow looked up, mildly astonished.

During a decade of intimacy these two men had joyously, affectionately and consistently insulted each other on all possible occasions. Now, however, there was a certain purposeful ring in Benton's voice which told the other this was quite different from the time-honored affectation of slander. Consequently his demand for further enlightenment came with terse directness.

Benton nodded and a defiant glint came to his pupils.

"I come to serve notice," he announced briefly, "of something I mean to do."

Van took the pipe from his mouth and regarded it with concentrated attention, while his friend went on in carefully gauged voice.

"I am here," he explained, "as a guest in your house. I mean to make war on certain plans and arrangements which presumably have your sympathy and support—and I mean to make the hardest war I know." He paused, but as Van gave no indication of cutting in, he went on in aggressive announcement. "What I mean to do is my business—mine and a girl's—but since she is your kinswoman and this is your place, it wouldn't be quite fair to begin without warning."

For a time Bristow's attitude remained that of deep and silent reflection. Finally he knocked the ashes from his pipe and came over until he stood directly confronting Benton.

"So she has told you?" was his brief question at last.

The other nodded.

The master of "Idle Times" paced thoughtfully up and down the room. When at length he stopped it was to clap his hand on his class-mate's shoulder.

"George," he said, with a voice hardened to edit down the note of sympathy that threatened it, "you seem to start out with the assumption that I am against you. Get that out of your head. Cara has hungered for freedom. We've felt that she had the right to, at least, her little intervals of recess. It happened that she could have them here. Here she could be Miss Carstow—and cease to be Cara of Maritzburg. I am sorry if you—and she—must pay for these vacations with your happiness. I see now that people who are sentenced to imprisonment, should not play with liberty."

"She is not going to play with liberty," declared Benton categorically. "She is going to have it. She is going to have for the rest of her life just what she wants." He lifted his hand in protest against anticipated interruption. "I know that you have got to line up with your royal relatives. I know the utter impossibility of what I want—but I'm going to win. If you regard me as a burglar, you may turn me out, but you can't stop me."

"I sha'n't turn you out," mused Van quietly. "I wish you could win. But you are not merely fighting people. You are fighting an idea. It is only for an idea that men and women martyr themselves. With Cara this idea has become morbid—an obsession. She has inherited it together with an abnormally developed courage, and her conception of courage is to face what she most hates and fears."

"But if I can show her that it is a mistaken courage—that instead of loyalty it is desertion?" The man spoke with quick eagerness.

Van shook his head, and his eyes clouded with the gravity of sympathy for a futile resolve.

"That you can't do. I am an American myself. I'm not policing thrones. To me it seems a monstrous thing that a girl superbly American in everything but the accident of birth should have no chance—no opportunity to escape life-imprisonment. It doesn't altogether compensate that the prison happens to be a palace."

For a time neither spoke, then Bristow went on.

"At the age of five, Cara stood before a mirror and critically surveyed herself. At the end of the scrutiny she turned away with a satisfied sigh. 'I finks I'm lovely,' she announced. At five one is frank. Her verdict has since then been duly and reliably confirmed by everyone who has known her—yet she might as well have been born into unbeautiful, hopeless slavery."

Benton went to the window and stood moodily looking out. Finally he wheeled to demand: "How did the crown of Maritzburg come to your uncle?"

"When he married my aunt," said Bristow, "he fancied himself safe-guarded from the ducal throne by two older brothers. That's why he was able to choose his own wife. He was dedicated with passionate loyalty to his brushes and paint tubes. He saw before him achievement of that sort. Assassination claimed his father and brothers, and, facing the same peril, he took up the distasteful duties of government. My aunt's life was intolerably shadowed by the terror of violence for him. She died at Cara's birth and the child inherited all the protest and acceptance so paradoxically bequeathed by her heart-broken mother."

"Realizing that Cara could not hope to escape a royal marriage, her father looked toward Galavia. There at least the strain was clean ... untouched by degeneracy and untainted with libertinism. Karyl is as decent a chap as yourself. He loves her, and though he knows she accepts him only from compulsion, he believes he can eventually win her love as well as her mere acquiescence. It's all as final as the laws of the Medes and Persians."

Again there was a long silence. Bristow began to wonder if it was, with his friend, the silence of despair and surrender. At last Benton lifted his face and his jaw was set unyieldingly.

"Personally," he commented quietly, "I have decided otherwise."

Despite the raw edge on the air, the hardier guests at "Idle Times" still clung to those outdoor sports which properly belonged to the summer.

That afternoon a canoeing expedition was made up river to explore a cave which tradition had endowed with some legendary tale of pioneer days and Indian warfare.

Pagratide, having organized the expedition with that object in view, had made use of his prior knowledge to enlist Cara for the crew of his canoe, but Benton, covering a point that Pagratide had overlooked, pointed out that an engagement to go up the river in a canoe is entirely distinct from an engagement to come down the river in a canoe. He cited so many excellent authorities in support of his contention that the matter was decided in his favor for the return trip, and Mrs. Porter-Woodleigh, all unconscious that her escort was a Crown Prince, found in him an introspective and altogether uninteresting young man.

Benton and the girl in one canoe, were soon a quarter of a mile in advance of the others, and lifting their paddles from the water they floated with the slow current. The singing voices of the party behind them came softly adrift along the water. All of the singers were young and the songs had to do with sentiment.

The girl buttoned her sweater closer about her throat. The man stuffed tobacco into the bowl of his pipe and bent low to kindle it into a cheerful spot of light.

A belated lemon afterglow lingered at the edge of the sky ahead. Against it the gaunt branches of a tall tree traced themselves starkly. Below was the silent blackness of the woods.

Suddenly Benton raised his head.

"I have a present for you," he announced.

"A present?" echoed the girl. "Be careful, Sir Gray Eyes. You played the magician once and gave me a rose. It was such a wonderful rose"—she spoke almost tenderly,—"that it has spoiled me. No commonplace gift will be tolerated after that."

"This is a different sort of present," he assured her. "This is a god."

"A what!" Cara was at the stern with the guiding paddle. The man leaned back, steadying the canoe with a hand on each gunwale, and smiled into her face.

"Yes," he said, "he is a god made out of clay with a countenance that is most unlovely and a complexion like an earthenware jar. I acquired him in the Andes for a few *centavos*. Since then we have been companions. In his day he had his place in a splendid temple of the Sun Worshipers. When I rescued him he was squatting cross-legged on a counter among silver and copper trinkets belonging to a civilization younger than his own. When you've been a god and come to be a souvenir of ruins and dead things—" the man paused for a moment, then with the ghost of a laugh went on, "—it makes you see things differently. In the twisted squint of his small clay face one reads slight regard for mere systems and codes."

He paused so long that she prompted him in a voice that threatened to become unsteady. "Tell me more about him. What is his godship's name?"

"He looked so protestingly wise," Benton went on, "that I named him Jonesy. I liked that name because it fitted him so badly. Jonesy is not conventional in his ideas, but his morals are sound. He has seen religions and civilizations and dynasties flourish and decay, and it has all given him a certain perspective on life. He has occasionally given me good council."

He paused again, but, noting that the singing voices were drawing nearer, he continued more rapidly.

"In Alaska I used to lie flat on my cot before a great open fire and his godship would perch cross-legged on my chest. When I breathed, he seemed to shake his fat sides and laugh. When a pagan god from Peru laughs at you in a Yukon cabin, the situation calls for attention. I gave attention.

"Jonesy said that the major human motives sweep in deep channels, full-tide ahead. He said you might in some degree regulate their floods by rearing abutments, but that when you try to build a dam to stop the Amazon you are dealing with folly. He argued that when one sets out to dam up the tides set flowing back in the tributaries of the heart it is written that one must fail. That is the gospel according to Jonesy."

He turned his face to the front and shot the canoe forward. There was silence except for the quiet dipping of their paddles, the dripping of the water from the lifted blades, and the song drifting down river. Finally Benton added:

"I don't know what he will say to you, but perhaps he will give you good advice—on those matters which the centuries can't change."

Cara's voice came soft, with a hint of repressed tears. "He has already given me good advice, dear—" she said, "good advice that I can't follow."

CHAPTER V

IT IS DECIDED TO MASQUERADE

The first day of quail-shooting found Van Bristow's guests afield.

Separated from the others, Benton and Cara came upon a small grove, like an oasis in the stretching acres of stubble. Under a scarlet maple that reared itself skyward all aflame, and shielded by a festooning profusion of wild-grape, a fallen beech-trunk offered an inviting seat. The girl halted and grounded arms.

The man seated himself at her feet and looked up. He framed a question, then hesitated, fearing the answer. Finally he spoke, controlling his voice with an effort.

"Cara," he questioned, "how long have I?"

Her eyes widened as if with terror. "A very—very little time, dear," she said. "It frightens me to think how little. Then—then—nothing but memory. Do you realize what it all means?" She leaned forward and laid a hand on each of his shoulders. "Just one week more, and after that I shall look out to sea when the sun sinks, red and sullen, into leaden waters and think of—of Arcady—and you."

"Don't, Cara!" He seized her hands and went on talking fast and vehemently. "Listen! I love you—that is not a unique thing. You love me—that is the miracle. And because of a distorted idea of duty, our lives must go to wreck. Don't you see the situation is ludicrous—intolerable? You are trying to live a medieval life in a day of wireless telegraph and air ships."

She nodded. "But what are we going to do about it?" she questioned simply.

"Cara, dear—if I could find a way!" he pleaded eagerly. "Suppose I could play the magician!"

He rose and stood back of the log.

She leaned back so that she might look into his eyes. "I wish you could," she mused with infinite weariness.

He stooped suddenly and kissed the drooping lips with a resentful sense of the monstrous injustice of a scheme of things wherein such lips could droop.

"No, no, no!" she cried. "You must not! I've got to be Queen of Galavia—I've got to be his wife." Then, in a quick, half-frightened tone: "Yet when you are with me I can't help it. It's wicked to love you—and I do."

He smiled through the misery of his own frown. "Am I so bad as that?" he questioned.

"You are so bad"—she suddenly caught his hands in hers and slowly shook her head—"that I don't trust myself on the same side of the road with you. You must go across and sit on that opposite side." She lightly kissed his forehead. "That's a kiss before exile—now go."

He measured the distance with disapproving eyes. "That must be fifteen feet away," he protested, "and my arms are not a yard long." He stretched them out, viewing them ruefully.

"Go!" she repeated with sternness.

He obeyed slowly, his face growing sullen.

"If I am to stay here until I recant what I said about your odious kingdom and your miserable throne, I'll—I'll—" He cast about for a sufficiently rebellious sentiment, then resolutely asserted: "I'll stay here until I rot in my chains." He raised his hands and shook imaginary manacles. "Clink! Clink! Clink!" he added dramatically.

"You are being punished for being too fascinating to a poor little fool princess who has played truant and who doesn't want to go back to school." She talked on with forced levity. "As for the kingdom,"—once more her eyes became wistful—"you may say what you like about it. You can't possibly hate it as much as I. There is no anarchist screaming his adherence to the red flag or inventing infernal machines, who hates all thrones as much as the one small girl who must needs be Queen of Galavia. No, *lèse-majesté* is not the fault for which you are being punished."

For a while he was silent, then his voice was raised in exile, almost cheerfully.

"Destiny is stronger than the paretic councils of little inbred kings. Why, Cara, I can get one good, husky Methodist preacher who can do in five minutes what I hardly think your royalties can undo—ever."

"Oh, don't!" she stopped him with plaintive appeal. "I know all that. I know it. Don't you realize that the longer the flight into the open blue of the skies, the harder the return to a gilt cage? But, dearest—there is such a thing as keeping one's parole. I must go back, unless I am held by a force stronger than I. I must go back. I have been here almost too long."

"Cara," he said slowly, "I, too, have a sense of duty. It is to you. The open blue of the skies is yours by right—divine right. You have nothing to do with cages, gilt or otherwise. My duty is to free you. I mean to do it. I haven't finished thinking it out yet, but I am going to find the way."

Her answering voice was deeply grave.

"If you just devise a situation where I shall have to fight it all out again, you will only make it harder for me. I must do what I must do. I could only be rescued by some power stronger than myself. Come, let's go back."

At dinner that same evening Mrs. Van announced to her guests that "by request of one who should be nameless," punctuating her pledge of secrecy with a pronounced glance at Benton, there would be a masquerade affair on the evening before Cara's departure for New York. She said this was to be an informal sort of frolic in fancy dress, and the only requirement would be that every grown-up should for an evening return to childhood.

On the next morning ensued a hegira from the place, the object whereof was guarded with the most diplomatic deception and secrecy.

"Why this unanimous desertion?" demanded Van indignantly from the head of the table when it began to develop that an exodus impended. "Do your appetites crave the stimulus of city cooking? Are you leaving my simple roof for the lobster palaces?"

Benton shook his head. "Singular," he commented, studying his grape-fruit with the air of an oracle gazing into crystal. "There, for example, is Colonel Centress who will probably tell you that he has had an imperative summons to confer with his brokers and—"

He paused, while the ancient beau across the table quickly nodded affirmation.

"Quite so. How did you guess it?" he inquired.

"Never talk business at table, of course, but this is a mysterious flurry in stocks—quite a mysterious flurry."

"Quite so," echoed Benton. "Nevertheless, if you were to shadow the gallant Colonel in Manhattan to-day he would probably lead you to a costuming tailor, where you would discover him in the act of being fitted with a Roman toga or a crusader's mail."

Mrs. Porter-Woodleigh shot a malicious glance at the tall foreigner whose emotionless face proved a constant irritation to her exuberant vivacity. "I understand, Colonel Von Ritz," she innocently suggested, "that you are to impersonate a polar bear."

The Galavian smiled deep in his eyes only; his lips remained sober. One would have said that he had not recognized the thrust. "I shall only remain myself," he replied. "I am allowed to be a looker-on in Venice."

Under her breath the widow confided to her next neighbor: "Ah! then it is true."

"What are *you* going to town for?" demanded Mrs. Van, looking accusingly at Benton, as that gentleman arose from the table.

"I should say," he laughingly responded, "that I am going to complete final arrangements for getting the Isis into commission, but nobody would believe me. You are all becoming so diplomatic of late!"

Von Ritz glanced up casually. "There is one very dangerous diplomacy—one very difficult to become accustomed to," he commented. "I allude to the American diplomacy of frankness."

"The *Isis*? To think I have never seen your yacht!" mused Cara. "And yet you are allowing me to cross on a steamer."

"If she could be put in shape so soon," declared Benton regretfully, glancing from Von Ritz to Pagratide, "I should shanghai Mrs. Van for a chaperon and give a party to Europe. Unfortunately I can't get her in readiness promptly enough; unless," he added hopefully, "Miss Carstow can postpone her sailing-day?"

CHAPTER VI

IN WHICH ROMEO BECOMES DROMIO

When Benton had straightened out his car for the run to the city, and the road had begun to slip away under the tires, he turned to McGuire, his chauffeur.

"McGuire," he inquired, "where is the runabout?"

"At 'Idle Times,' sir. You loaned it to Mr. Bristow to fill up the garage."

"I remember. Now, listen!" And as Benton talked a slow grin of contentment spread across the visage of Mr. McGuire, hinting of some enterprise that appealed to his venturesome soul with a lure beyond the ordinary.

In the city, Benton was a busy man, though his visit to the costumer's was brief. Coming out of the place, he fancied he caught a glimpse of Von Ritz, but the view was fleeting and he decided that his eyes must have deceived him. He had himself patronized a rather obscure shop, recommended by Mr. McGuire. Von Ritz would presumably have selected some more fashionable purveyor of disguises even had his assertion that he would not masquerade been made only to deceive. Perhaps, thought the American, Colonel Von Ritz was becoming an obsession with him, merely because he stood for Galavia and the threat of royalty's mandate. He was convinced of this later in the day, when he once more fancied that a disappearing pair of broad shoulders belonged to the European. This time he laughed at the idea. The surroundings made the supposition ludicrous. It was among the tawdry shops of ship chandlers in the East Side, where he himself had gone in search of certain able seamen in the company of the sailing-master of the *Isis.* Von Ritz would hardly be consorting with the fo'castle men who frequent the water front below Brooklyn Bridge.

The few days of the last week raced by, with all the charm of sky and field that the magic of Indian summer can lavish, and for Benton and Cara, they raced also with the sense of fast-slipping hope and relentlessly marching doom. Outwardly Cara set a pace for vivacious and care-free enjoyment that left Mrs. Porter-Woodleigh, the "semi-professional light-hearted lady," as O'Barreton named her, "to trail along in the ruck." Alone with Benton, there was always the furrow between the brows and the distressed gaze upon the mystery beyond the sky-line, but Pagratide and Von Ritz were vigilant, to the end that their tête-à-têtes were few.

Neither Benton nor Cara had alluded to the man's overbold assertion that he would find a way. It was a futile thing said in eagerness. The day of the dance, the last day they could hope for together, came unprefaced by development. To-morrow she must take up her journey and her duty: her holiday would be at its end. It was all the greater reason why this evening should be memorable. He should think of her afterward as he saw her to-night, and it pleased her that in the irresponsibility of the maskers she should appear to him in the garb of vagabond liberty, since in fact freedom was impossible to her.

As the kaleidoscope of the first dance sifted and shifted its pattern of color, three men stood by the door, scanning the disguised figures with watchful eyes.

One of the three was fantastically arrayed as a cannibal chief, in brown fleshings, with cuffs upon his ankles, gaudy decorations about his neck, and huge rings in nose and ears.

The second man was a Bedouin: a camel-driver of the Libyan Desert. From the black horsehair circlet on his temples a turban-scarf fell to his shoulders. He was wrapped in a brown cashmere cloak which dropped domino-like to his ankles. Shaggy brows ran in an unbroken line from temple to temple, masking his eyes, while a fierce mustache and beard obliterated the contour of his lower face. His cheek-bones and forehead showed, under some dye, as dark as leather, and as his gaze searchingly raked the crowds, he fingered a string of Moslem prayer-beads.

The third man was conspicuous in ordinary dress. Save for the decoration of the Order of Takavo, suspended by a crimson ribbon on his shirt-front, and the Star of Galavia, on the left lapel of his coat, there was no break in the black and white scheme of his evening clothes. Von Ritz had told the truth. He was not disguised. He stood, his arms folded on his breast, towering above the Fiji Islander, possibly a quarter of an inch taller than the Bedouin. A half-amused smile lurked in his steady eyes—the smile of unwavering brows and dispassionately steady mouth-line.

The cannibal chief waved his hand. "Bright the lamps shone o'er fair women and brave men!" he declaimed, in a disguised voice; then scowled about him villainously, remembering that an affable quoting of Lord Byron is incompatible with the qualities of a man-eating savage.

The Bedouin gravely inclined his head. "*Allahu Akbar!*" he responded, in a soft voice.

Suddenly the caravan driver commenced a hurried and zigzag course across the crowded floor. The eyes of Colonel Von Ritz indolently followed.

Through a low-silled window a girl had just entered, carrying herself with the untrammeled freedom of some wild thing, erect, poised from the waist, rhythmic in motion. Her walk was like the scansion of good verse. The Bedouin caught the grace before the ensemble of costume met his eye. It was in harmony.

She wore a silk skirt to the ankles, and about her waist and hips was bound the yellow and red sash of the Spanish gipsy, tightly knotted, and falling at its tasseled ends. Her arms were bare to the elbows, and gay with bracelets; her hair fell from her forehead and temples, dropping over her shoulders in two ribbon bound braids. A tall, gray-cowled monk, whose military bearing gave the lie to his cassock, a Spanish grandee, and a fool in motley saw her at the same moment and hurried to intercept her, but with a slide which carried him a quarter of the way across the floor the Bedouin arrived first, and before the others had come up he was drifting away with her in the tide of the dancers.

"Allah is good to me—Flamencine," whispered the camel-driver as he drew her close to avoid a careless dancer.

"Why, Flamencine?" demanded a carefully altered voice, from which, however, the music had not been eliminated.

"Don't you remember?" The Arab stole a covert, identifying glance down at the tip of one ear which showed under its masking of brown hair—an ear that looked as though it were chiseled from the pink coral of Capri. He quoted:

"'There was a gipsy maiden within the forest green,

There was a gipsy maiden who shook a tambourine.

The stars of night had not the face,

The woodland wind had not the grace,

Of Flamencine.'"

Then the music stopped, and with its silencing came the monk, the clown, the grandee, and others.

In the insistent demand of the many the Arab had too few dances with the Spanish girl. There were Comanches, Samurai, policemen, Zulus and courtiers, who, seeing her dance, discovered that their immediate avocation was dancing with her.

Yet it wanted an hour of unmasking time when a Bedouin led a gipsy maiden from Andalusia into the deserted library, where the darkness was broken only by blazing logs on an open hearth.

When they were alone he turned to her anxiously. His voice was freighted with appeal. Her face, now unmasked, wore an expression of stunned misery.

"Dear," he asked, "how are you?"

She gazed at the flickering logs. "I should think you would know," she answered wearily. Then, with a mirthless laugh, she spread both hands toward the blaze. "I'm looking ahead—I can see it all there in the fire." Her fingers convulsively clenched themselves until blue marks showed against the pink palms.

He pushed a chair forward for her, but with a shake of her head she declined it.

"Whoever heard of a gipsy girl sitting in a leather chair?" she demanded. "It's more like—like some effete princess."

She dropped to the Persian rug and, gathering her knees between her clasped hands, sat looking into the dying blaze. "For a few brief minutes I am the gipsy girl," she added.

"And," he said, dropping cross-legged to the rug at her side, "when the caravan halts at evening, and prayers have been said facing Mecca, and the grunting camels kneel, to be unloaded, neither do we, the gipsies of the desert, sit in chairs." He swayed slightly toward her, lowering his voice to a whisper. As the soft touch of her shoulder brushed him and electrified him, his cashmere-draped arms closed around her and held her hungrily to him. The vagrant maiden of Andalusia and the caravan-driver of Africa sat gazing together at the glowing pictures in the logs as they turned slowly to ashes.

"Cara," he went on in a voice of pent-up earnestness, "we be nomads—we two. 'The scarlet of the maples can shake us like the cry of bugles going by.' Come away with me while there is time. Let us follow out our destinies where gipsy blood calls us; in the desert, the jungle, wherever you say. Let your fancy be our guide—your heart our compass. Suppose"—he paused and, with one outstretched arm, pointed to the fire—"suppose that to be a camp-fire—what do you see in the coals?"

"I have already told you," she said wearily. "I see a throne, a life with all the confining littleness of a prison, with none of the breadth of an empire. I see the sacrifice of all I love. I see year upon year of purple desolation.... Purple is the color of mourning and royalty."

She fell silent, and he spoke slowly.

"I see the desert, many-hued, like an opal with the setting of the sun. I see the flickering of camp-fires and the palm-fringe of an oasis. I see the tapering minarets of a mosque, and the long booths of the bazaars. I smell the scent of the perfume-seller's stall, the heavy sweetness of attar of roses.... I hear the tinkle of camel bells.... There comes a change.... I see a mountain-pass and a mule-train crawling through the dust, I see the paths that go around the world. Which of our pictures do you prefer?"

She gave a pained, low cry, and buried her face passionately on his shoulder. "Oh, you know, you know!" she cried, in a piteous voice. "And you love me, yet you tempt me to break my parole. If I could do it and be freed of the responsibility! If a miracle could work itself!"

"Cara," he whispered, resolutely steadying himself, "don't forget the gospel according to Jonesy. You can't dam up the tributaries of the heart. Some day you must come to me. That much is immutably written. For God's sake come now while the road is still clear. Otherwise we shall grope our ways to each other, even if it be through tragedy—through hell itself."

For a moment she gazed at him with wide eyes.

"I know it—" she whispered in a frightened voice. "I know it—and yet I must go ahead."

He rose and lifted her; then as she stood clinging to him he said: "I ask your forgiveness if I've made it harder—and one boon. Slip away with me and give me an hour with you."

"They will find me. Pagratide and Von Ritz will find me," she objected helplessly. "They won't let us be alone for long."

"Listen," he replied. "It is not too cold and the moon is brilliant. It is the last real moon for me. Come with me in my car for a while."

"You must not make love to me," she stipulated. "I am going to try to get my face properly composed—and if you make love to me, I can't. Besides, when you make love I'm rather afraid of you. So you mustn't."

Then, with a wild spasmodic gesture, she caught the edges of his cashmere cloak and gripped them tightly in both hands as she looked up into his eyes and impetuously contradicted herself.

"Yes, please do," she appealed.

He laughed. "Destiny says I must make love to you," he asserted, "and who am I to disobey Destiny?"

Outside, she insisted upon waiting by the bridge while he went for his car. So he turned and started alone to the point on the driveway just around the angle of the house, where McGuire, pursuant to previous orders, was to be waiting with the machine. It had been only an hour since Benton had slipped away from the dancers and consulted with McGuire in the shadow of the wall, instructing him explicitly in his duties. McGuire was to wait with the machine ready upon call. The lamps were not to be lighted. When Benton came, the chauffeur was to run the car to the point where a lady should enter it. He was at that point to leave, without words. It had been impressed on McGuire that utter silence was imperative. The chauffeur was then to follow in the runabout, acting as a reserve in the event of need. Both cars were to take a certain circuitous route to a point on the shore thirty miles distant, the runabout keeping just close enough to hold the first car in sight. McGuire had listened and understood. Yet now McGuire was missing, together with one very necessary motor-car.

As Benton stood, boiling with wrath at the miscarriage of his plans, he fancied he heard the soft muffled song of his motor just beyond the turn where the road circled the house. He bent and held a lighted match close to the gravel. On a muddied spot he found the easily recognizable tread of his tires. The car had been there. For the sake of speed he ran to the garage near by and took a swift look at the runabout. It was waiting, and, thanks to the God of Machines, would start on compression. He flung himself to the driver's seat and gave it the spark. Far away—about as far as the bridge, he calculated—he heard one short, cautious blast of an automobile horn.

Just before the last turn brought him to the bridge, where he should meet Cara, he noticed a man hurrying toward him, on foot, and recognized McGuire. Totally mystified, he slowed down the machine.

"Get in, you infernal blockhead," he called. "Tell me about it as we go. I'm in a hurry."

But McGuire performed strangely. He clapped one hand to his forehead and looked at his employer out of large, wild eyes. "Am I dippy? My God! Am I dippy?" he exclaimed, repeating the question over and over in a low, trembling voice.

"Apparently you are. Get in, damn you!" Benton ordered.

"It's weird," declared McGuire. "It's damned weird."

"Why, sir," he ran on, talking fast, now that the first shock was over and his tongue again loosened. "Either I've made a fool mistake, or else I'm crazier than hell. I waited at the place you said. You—or your ghost—came and took his seat, and waved his hand. I started the car for the bridge. He didn't say a word. At the bridge I jumped out. He was you—and yet you are here—same size—same costume—same beard—even the same beads around the neck."

They had almost reached the bridge and were slowing down when Benton, scanning the road, empty in the moonlight, grasped for the first time a definite suspicion of what had happened.

"Cara!" he shouted. "Good God, where is she?"

The chauffeur leaned over and shouted into his ear. "I'm telling you, sir. The lady's in that other car—with that other edition of you. And, sir—beggin' your pardon—they're beatin' it like hell!"

Benton's only answer was to feed gas to the spark so frantically that the car seemed to rise from the ground and shiver before it settled again. Then it shot forward and reeled crazily into a speed never intended for a curving road at night.

The moonlight fell on a gray streak of a car, driven by a maniac with a scarf blowing back from a turban over two wildly gleaming eyes.

Back at "Idle Times" a Capuchin monk, wandering apart from the dancers in consonance with the austere proclaiming of his garb, was studying the frivolous gamboling of a school of fountain gold-fish in the conservatory. He looked up, scowling, to take a note from a servant.

"Colonel Von Ritz said to hand this to the gentleman masquerading as a monk," explained the man.

"Von Ritz," growled the monk. "He annoys me."

He impatiently tore open the letter and scanned it. His brows contracted in astonished mystification, then slowly his eyes narrowed and kindled.

The scrawl ran:

"Your Highness: If you see neither Mr. Benton, masquerading as an Arab, her Highness, the Princess, nor myself in ten minutes from the time of receiving this, take the car which you will find ready in the garage. My orderly will be there to act as your chauffeur. Follow the main road to the second village. Turn there to the right, and drive to the small bay, where you will find me or an explanation. I have been conducting certain investigations. The affair is urgent and touches matters of great import to Europe as well us to Your Highness."

CHAPTER VII

IN WHICH DROMIO BECOMES ROMEO

When Cara, waiting at the bridge, had seen the car flash up, a bearded Bedouin at the wheel, she had leaped lightly to the seat beside him, without waiting for the machine to come to a full stop; then she had thrown herself back luxuriously on the cushions with a sigh of satisfaction, and had only said: "Drive me fast."

For a long time she lay back, drinking, in long draughts, the spiced night air, frosted only enough to give it flavor. There was no necessity for speech, and above, the stars glittered lavishly, despite the white light of the moon.

At last she murmured half-aloud and almost contentedly: "'Who knows but the world may end to-night?'"

Above the throbbing purr of the engine which had already done ten miles, the man beside her caught the voice, but missed the words. He bent forward.

"I beg your pardon?" he politely inquired.

At the question she started violently, and both hands came to her heart with a spasmodic movement. Von Ritz carried the car around an ugly rut.

"Don't be alarmed, Your Highness," he said, in a cold, evenly modulated voice which, though pitched low, carried clearly above the noise of the cylinders. "I may call you 'Your Highness' now, may I not? We are quite alone. Or do you still prefer that I respect your incognita?"

The girl's eyes blazed upon him until he could feel their intense focusing, though he kept his own fixed unbendingly on the road ahead. Finally she mastered her anger enough to speak.

"Colonel Von Ritz," she commanded, "you will take me back at once!" She drew herself as far away from him as the space on the seat permitted.

"Your Highness's commands are supreme." The man spoke in the same even voice. "I intend taking Your Highness back—when it is safer for Your Highness to go back."

He turned the car suddenly to the right and sped along the narrower road that led away from the main thoroughfare.

"You will take me back, now. I had not supposed that to a gentleman—" Her voice choked into silence and her eyes filled with angry tears.

"Your Highness misunderstands," he said coldly. "I obey the throne. If I live long enough to serve it in another reign, Your Highness will be Your Majesty. Yet even then will your commands be no more supreme to me—no more sacred—than now. But even then, Your Highness—"

"Call me Miss Carstow," she interrupted in impassioned anger. "I will have my freedom for to-night at least."

"Yet even then, Miss Carstow," he calmly resumed, "when danger threatens you or your throne, I shall take such means as I can to avert that danger, as I am doing now. Even though"—for a moment the cold, metallic evenness left his voice and a human note stole into his words—"even though the reward be contempt."

She did not answer.

"Your High—Miss Carstow,"—Von Ritz spoke with a deferential finality—"believe me, some things are inevitable."

Suddenly the car stopped.

The girl made a movement as though she would rise, but the man's arm quietly stretched itself across before her, not touching her, but forming an effective barrier.

She did not speak, but her eyes blazed indignantly. For the first time he was able to return her gaze directly, and as she looked into the unflinching gray pupils, under the level brows, there was a momentary combat, then her own dropped. He sat for a space with his arm outstretched, holding her prisoner in the seat.

"Your Highness"—he spoke as impersonally as a judge ruling from the bench—"I must remind you again that I am your escort to-night only in order that someone else may not be. What his plans were, I need not now say, but I know, and it became my duty to thwart him. It is hardly necessary to explain how I discovered Mr. Benton's purpose. It was not easy, but it has been accomplished. I have acquainted myself with his movements, his intention, and his preparations; I have even counterfeited his masquerade and stolen his car. There are bigger things at stake than individual wishes. I stand for the throne. Mr. Benton has played a daring game—and lost."

He paused, and she found herself watching with a strange fascination the face almost marble-like in its steadiness.

"Some day—perhaps soon," he went on, the arm unmoved, "you will be Queen of Galavia." She shuddered. "You can then strip away my epaulets if you choose. For the moment, however, I must regard you as a prisoner of war and ask your parole, as a gentleman and an officer, not to leave the car while I investigate the trouble with the motor. Otherwise—" he added composedly, "we shall have to remain as we are."

She hesitated, her chin thrown up and her eyes blazing; then, with a glance at the unmoving arm, she bowed reluctant assent.

"All I promise is to remain in the car," she said. "May I go back into the tonneau?"

Satisfying himself that the engine was temporarily dead, he responded, with a half-smile, "That promise I think is sufficient."

He bent to his task of diagnosis. After much futile spinning of the crank, he rose and contemplated the stalled engine.

"Since this machine went out with lamps unlighted, and I have no matches in this garb, I must go to that farmhouse up the hillside—where the light shines through the trees—. Will Your Highness regard your parole as effective until my return, not to leave the car? Yes? I thank Your Highness; I shall not be long."

The girl for answer honked the horn in several loud blasts, and he stopped with a murmured apology to silence it by tearing off the bulb and throwing it to one side.

The Colonel turned and took his way through the woods, statuesquely upright and spectral in his long Arab cloak.

Benton and McGuire had just passed the crossing where Von Ritz had left the main road, when McGuire's quick ear caught the familiar tooting of the other horn and brought his hand to his employer's arm. The car was stopped, and McGuire, by match-light, examined the road with its frosty mud unmarked by fresh automobile tracks, save those running back from their own tires.

The runabout turned and slipped along cautiously to the rear, watchful for byways. At the cross-road McGuire was out again. His match, held close to the mud and gravel, revealed the tread of familiar tires.

"All right, sir," he briefly reported. "The other edition went this track."

With a twist of the wheel Benton was again on the trail. Back in the side lane stood a car in which a girl sat alone, solemnly indignant.

"Cara!" Benton was standing on the step. His voice was tremulous with solicitude and perplexed anxiety. "Cara!" he repeated. "What does it mean?"

"I don't know," she responded coolly. "Something seems to be broken."

"I don't mean that." McGuire was already investigating. "What does it mean?"

She sighed wearily.

"When I foolishly agreed to play Juliet to your Romeo," she informed him, and her tones were frigid, "I didn't know that your Romeo was really only a Dromio. The other edition of you"—he flinched at the words, and McGuire choked violently—"is back there, I believe, hunting for matches."

"She's all right, sir," interrupted McGuire in triumph. "She'll travel now. It's only disconnected spark plugs and a short circuiting."

"Travel, then!" snapped Benton. "Leave the runabout here. The other gentleman may prefer not to walk home."

As he swung himself into the tonneau, the chauffeur had already seized the wheel and the car was backing for the turn. Far back up the hillside there was a crashing of underbrush. A spectral figure, struggling with the unaccustomed drapery of a Bedouin robe, emerged from the woods into the open, and halted in momentary astonishment.

"I believe I am under parole—to the other Dromio—not to run away," she suggested wearily.

"Oh, that's all right; I'm doing this and I have no treaty with Galavia," replied the gentleman pleasantly. "Hit her up a bit, McGuire."

He took one of the hands that lay wearily in Cara's lap and she did not withdraw it. She only lay back in the leather upholstery and said nothing. Finally he bent nearer.

"Dearest," he said. There was no answer.

"Dearest," he whispered again.

She only turned her head and smiled forgiveness.

"What is the matter?" he asked.

"Oh, I'm so tired—so tired of all of it," she sighed. "Don't you see? I wish someone bigger than I am would take me away to a place where they had never heard of a throne—somewhere beyond the Milky Way."

He took her in his arms, and the spangle-crowned gipsy head fell heavily on his shoulder. She stretched up both arms towards the stars, and the moonlight glinted from her gilt bracelets.

"Somewhere beyond the Milky Way," she murmured, then collapsed like a tired child and lay still.

"Dearest," he whispered, "I'll tell you a secret." He paused and listened to the rhythmic cylinders throbbing a racing pulse; he looked back at the white band of road that was being flung out behind them like thread from a falling spool. He held her fiercely to him and kissed her. "I'll tell you a secret. You are being stolen. The *Isis* is waiting in a little cove, and there is steam in her engines, and a chaplain on board. If it's necessary I shall run up the skull and cross-bones at her masthead. Do you hear?" Then, with a less piratical voice: "Dearest, I love you."

She looked up drowsily into his eyes. "You don't have to be such a boa-constrictor," she suggested. "You are not a cave-man, after all, you know, if you *are* taking a lady without asking her." Then she contentedly whispered: "I'm going to sleep." And she did.

As the car at last swept around a curve and took the shore road, Benton caught, far away as yet, the red and green glint of tiny port and starboard lights on the bridge of the *Isis*, and the long ruby and emerald shafts quivering beneath in the calm waters of the bay. In the light of a low moon, swinging down the midnight sky, the trim silhouette of the yacht stood out boldly.

Cara, after sleeping through the rowboat stage of the journey, awoke on the deck of the *Isis* and gazed wonderingly about. In her ears was the sound of anchor chains upon the capstan.

"Is it a dream?" she asked.

"It is a dream to me, but I am going to make it real," he responded.

She went to the rail. He followed her.

"I shouldn't have let you, but I was so tired," she said, "I hardly knew where the dream began and the reality ended. Ah, I wish the dream could come true."

"This one is to come true, Cara," he whispered.

She shook her head. "Stand still!" she commanded.

He was bending forward with his elbows on the rail. Suddenly, with something like a stifled sob, she caught his head in both arms and held him close, so close that he heard her heart pounding and her breath coming with spasmodic gasps. He put out his arms, but she held him off.

"No, no; don't touch me now—only listen!"

He waited a moment before she spoke again.

"You said I was your prisoner." Her voice dropped in a tremor as though the tears would prevail, but she steadied it and went on. "I wish I were. Always I am your prisoner, but I must go back. It is because it is written."

He straightened up and took her in his arms. "I know how you have settled it," he said, "but I have stolen you. The anchor is coming up. You love me—I have claimed what is mine. It is now beyond your power, your responsibility."

"No, it is not," she softly denied. "I will not marry you—but I love you—I love you!"

"You mean that if I hold you my prisoner you will still not be my wife?" he incredulously demanded.

Slowly she nodded her head.

The man gazed off with the eyes of one stunned and slowly fought himself back into control before he trusted his voice. After a while, he raised his face and spoke in fragmentary sentences, his voice pitched low, his words broken.

"But you said—just now—back there on the road—you wished someone stronger than yourself—would take you away somewhere—beyond the Milky Way."

His tones strengthened and suddenly he almost sang out with recovered resolution, speaking buoyantly and triumphantly.

"Dearest, I am stronger than you, and I'm going to take you away—I'm going to take you beyond the Milky Way, to the uttermost stars of Love. How can it matter to me how far, if you are there?"

Again she shook her head.

"No, dear," she whispered, "you are not so strong as I, in this, because I am strong enough to say No when my heart says only Yes—and because Fate is stronger than any of us."

"Boat ahoy!" came a voice from the crow's nest.

"They have come for you," he said, speaking as through a fog. "Show them here," he shouted to an officer who was hurrying to the gangway.

Two figures came over the side, and slowly followed the first officer forward. One was a Capuchin monk, bearing himself rigidly; at his side strode a Bedouin, bedraggled, but erect and military of bearing. The original Arab turned with a sudden sag of the shoulders and looked helplessly out at the path of silver that stretched across the water below, to the moon, now sunk close to the horizon. He waved one hand in a gesture of submission and despair, and stood silent.

The gipsy girl, standing near, took a sudden step forward and stood close to him us the others approached.

"They may take me back if they wish to, now," she said, with a suddenly upflaring defiance. "But they shall find me like this!" And she flung her arms about his neck and kissed him.

CHAPTER VIII

THE PRINCESS CONSULTS JONESY

The coldness of the moonlight killed the pallor of Karyl's face, but added a note of stark accentuation to his set chin and labored self-containment. Von Ritz, despite his bedraggled masquerade was as composed and expressionless as though he had seen nothing beyond the expected. With Von Ritz nothing was beyond the expected.

He had to-night counterfeited Benton's disguise; stolen Benton's car; substituted himself for the American and made a decisive effort to interrupt the kidnaping of a Queen.

Finding himself checkmated, he had joined forces with the Prince and brought the pursuit to a successful termination. His manner now was precisely what it had been last night, when his only excitement had been a game of billiards. Men who knew him would have told you that his manner had been the same on a certain red and smoky day when the order of Takavo had been pinned on his breast, in the reek and noise of a battlefield.

After a moment of tense silence, Benton took a step forward.

"At any suitable time," he said, in a voice too low for Cara to catch, "I shall, of course, be entirely at your service."

Pagratide drew a labored breath, but when he raised his head it was to lift his brows inquiringly.

"For what?" he asked in an equally low tone. "Have I asked any questions?" In a matter-of-fact voice he added: "It is growing late. If Miss Carstow has finished the inspection of your yacht, I suggest a return."

Benton recognized the other's refusal to read his motive. After all that was the best course; the only course. Pagratide stepped forward.

"Mr. Benton had the pleasure of driving you down—" he suggested, "may I have the same honor, returning?"

The girl met the eyes of the Prince, with defiance in her own.

"I am not a child!" she vehemently declared. "We may as well be honest with each other. If he had chosen to have it so, you could not have come aboard. I must obey the decrees of State!" She paused, then impulsively swept on: "I can force myself to do what I must do, but I cannot compel my heart—that is his, utterly his." She raised both hands. "Now you know," she said. "You may decide."

Karyl inclined his head.

"I have questioned nothing," he repeated. "Will you honor me by returning in my car?"

Cara tilted her chin rebelliously.

"No," she said, "I don't think I shall. My vacation ends to-morrow if you still wish it, but to-night it has not ended. I return with Mr. Benton."

Pagratide stiffened painfully, but with supreme self-mastery he forced a smile as though he had asked nothing more than a dance—and had found it engaged.

"I must submit," he replied in a steady voice. "I even understand. But you will agree with me that they"—with a gesture toward the direction from which they had come—"had best know nothing."

Benton and Von Ritz went to the gangway, where the yachtsman bent forward to give some direction to the boat crew below.

"Karyl!" The girl moved impulsively toward the man she must marry, and laid a hand on his arm. "Karyl," she said plaintively, "if you only wanted to marry me for State reasons—it would be different. It wouldn't hurt me then to hurt you. You mean so much as a friend, but I can never be in love with you. You are being unfair with yourself—if you go on. I must be honest with you."

Pagratide spoke slowly, and his voice carried the tremor of feeling.

"You have always been honest with me, and I will make you love me. Until you marry me I have no privilege to question you. When you do, I shall not have to question you." He leaned forward and spoke confidently. "I would marry you if you hated me—and then I would win your love!"

An hour later the Spanish gipsy girl, having shown herself in the emptying ball-room with ingenious excuses for her long absence, took refuge in her own apartments.

On sailing day, Benton, at the pier, watched the steamer stand out into the river between the coming and going of ferry-boats and tugs. About him stamped the usual farewell throng with hats raised and handkerchiefs a-flutter. The music of the ship's band grew faint as a wider and wider gap of water opened between the wharf and the liner's gray hull.

Gradually the crowd scattered back through the great barn-like spaces of the pier-house to be re-absorbed by cabs, motors and surface-cars into the main arteries of the city's life. It was over. *Bon voyage* had been said. One more ship had put out to sea.

Benton stood looking after a slim figure in a blue traveling gown and dark furs, pressed against the after-rail, her handkerchief waving in the raw wind. Most of the sea-going ones had retreated into the shelter of the saloon or cabin, but she remained.

Van Bristow, shivering at his friend's elbow, did not suggest turning back.

Cara stood, still looking shoreward, a furrow between her brows, her checks pale, her fingers tightly gripping the rail. She was holding with that grip to all her shaken self-command.

She saw the fang-edged skyline of lower Manhattan lifting its gray shafts through wet streamers of fog; she saw flotillas of squat ferry-boats shouldering their ways against the sullen heave of the river's tide-water; she heard the discordant shriek of their steam throats; she saw the tilting swoop of a hundred gulls, buffeting the wind; but she was conscious only of the vista of oily water widening between herself and him.

Von Ritz had long since drifted into the smoking-room where the men were christening the voyage with brandy-and-soda and dropping into tentative groups, regardful of future poker games.

Pagratide, at Cara's elbow, was silent, respecting her silence.

When at last the two had the deck to themselves and Manhattan had become a shadowy and ragged monotone, she turned and smiled. It was a smile of accepting the inevitable. He went with her to the forward deck where her staterooms were situated, and left her there in silence.

Von Ritz, standing apart near the threshold of the smokeroom, heard his name paged almost before the speaker had entered the door, and turned to take from the hand of the bearer a Marconigram just relayed from shore. He read it and for an instant a look of pain crossed the features that rarely yielded to expression. Then he sought out Karyl's stateroom.

Karyl turned wearily from the wintry picture of a sullenly heaving sea, to answer the rap on the door. His face did not brighten as he recognized Von Ritz.

The Colonel was that type of being upon whom men may depend or whom they must fear. Whenever there was need, Karyl had come to know that there would be Von Ritz, but also there went with him an austerity and an impersonality that robbed him of the gratitude and love he might have claimed.

Now there was a note almost surly in the expression with which the Prince looked up to greet his father's confidential representative.

"Well?" he demanded.

For answer the officer held out the message.

Karyl puckered his brows over the intricacies of the code and handed it back.

"Be good enough to construe it," he commanded.

"The King," said Von Ritz, "is ill. His Majesty wishes to instruct you in certain matters before—" He broke off with something like a catch in his voice, then continued calmly. "Recovery is despaired of, though death may not be immediate."

Karyl turned away, not wishing the soldier to see the tears he felt in his eyes, and Von Ritz discreetly withdrew as far as the door. There he paused, and after a moment's hesitation inquired:

"Her Highness goes to Maritzburg—to her father's Court—I presume?"

With his back still turned, the Prince nodded. "Why?" he demanded.

"Because—the message holds no hope—" Von Ritz paused, then added quietly "—and if Your Highness is called upon to mount the throne, it is advisable to hasten the marriage."

He backed out, closing the door behind him.

In her own cabin the girl had bolted the door. At the small desk of her *suite-de-luxe* she sat with her head on her crossed arms. For a half-hour she remained motionless.

Finally she rose and, with uncertain hands, opened a suitcase, drawing from its place among filmy fabrics and feminine essentials a small, squat figure of time-corroded clay. The little Inca *huaca* had perhaps looked with that same unseeing squint upon Princesses of other dynasties so long dead that their heartbreaks and ecstasies were now the same—nothing.

She placed the image before her and rested her chin on one hand, gazing at its grotesque and ancient visage.

Her eyes slowly filled with tears. Again she dropped her face on her arms and the tears overflowed.

Benton and Bristow had been sitting without speech as their motor threaded its way through the traffic along Fourteenth Street, and it was not until the chauffeur had turned north on Fifth Avenue that either spoke. Then Benton roused himself out of seeming lethargy to inquire with suddenness: "Do you remember the bull-fight we saw in Seville?"

His companion looked up, suppressing his surprise at a question so irrelevant.

"You mean the Easter Sunday performance," he asked, "when that negligent *banderillero* was gored?"

"Just so," assented Benton. "Do you remember the chap we met afterwards at one of the cafés? He was being fêted and flattered for the brilliancy of his work in the ring. His name was Blanco."

"Sure I remember him." Van talked glibly, pleased that the conversation had turned into channels so impersonal. "He was a fine-looking chap with the grace of a Velasquez dancing-girl and the nerve of a bull-terrier. I remember he was more like a grandee than a *toreador*. We had him dine with us—hard bread—black olives—fish—bad wine—all sorts of native truck. For the rest of our stay in Seville he was our inseparable companion. Do you remember how the street gamins pointed us out? Why, it was like walking down Broadway with your arm linked in that of Jim Jeffries!"

He paused, somewhat disconcerted by his companion's steady gaze; then, taking a fresh start, he went on, talking fast.

"Besides sticking bulls, he could discuss several topics in several languages. I recall that he had been educated for the Church. If he hadn't felt the lure of the strenuous life, he might have been celebrating Mass instead of playing guide for us. In the end he'd have won a cardinal's hat."

The fixity of the other's stare at last chilled and quelled his chatter to an embarrassed silence. He realized that the object of his mild subterfuge was transparent.

"I'm after his address—not his biography," suggested Benton coolly. "His name was Manuel Blanco, wasn't it?"

"Why, yes, I believe it was. What do you want with him?"

"Never mind that," returned his friend. "Do you happen to know where he lived? I seem to recall that you promised to write him frequent letters."

"By Jove, so I did," acknowledged Van with humility. "I must get busy. He is a good sort. His address—" He paused to search through his pocket-book for a small tablet dedicated to names and numbers, then added: "His address is *Numero 18, Calle Isaac Peral*, Cadiz."

Benton was scribbling the direction on the back of an envelope.

"You needn't grow penitent and start a belated correspondence," he suggested. "I am going to write him myself—and I'm going to visit him."

CHAPTER IX

THE TOREADOR APPEARS

Slowly, with a gesture almost subconscious, Benton slipped an unopened envelope from his breast pocket; turned it over; looked at it and slipped it back, still unopened. Then, leaning heavily on his elbow, he gazed off, frowning, over the rail of the yacht's forward deck.

The waters that lap the quays and wharves of Old Cadiz, green as jade and quiet as farm-yard pools, were darkening into inkiness toward shore. White walls that had been like ivory were turning into ashy gray behind the *Bateria San Carlos* and the pillars of the *Entrada.* The molten sun was sinking into a rich orange sky beyond the Moorish dome and Christian towers of the cathedral.

Shafts of red and green wavered and quaked in the black dock waters.

Between the hulks of cork- and salt-freighters, the steam yacht *Isis* slipped with as graceful a motion as that of the gulls. Then when the anchor chains ran gratingly out, Benton turned on his heel and went to his cabin.

Behind a bolted door he dropped into a chair and sat motionless. Finally the right hand wandered mechanically to his breast pocket and brought out the envelope. He read for the thousandth time the endorsement in the corner.

"Not to be opened until the evening of March 5th," and under that, "I love you."

There was another envelope; an outer one much rubbed from the pocket. It was directed in her hand and the blurred postmark bore a date in February. He could have described every mark upon the enclosing cover with the precision of a careful detective. When his impatient fingers had first torn off the end, only to be confronted by the order: "Not to be opened until the evening of March 5th," he had fallen back on studying outward marks and indications. In the first place, it had been posted from Puntal, and instead of the familiar violet stamp of Maritzburg, with which her other letters had been franked during the two months past, this stamp was pink, and its medallion bore the profile of Karyl.

That she had left Maritzburg, and that she had written him a message to be sealed for a month, meant that the date of March 5th had significance. That she was in Galavia meant that the significance was—he winced.

On the calendar of a bronze desk-set, the first four days of March were already cancelled. Now, taking up a blue pencil, he crossed off the number five. After that he looked at his watch. It wanted one minute of six. He held the timepiece before him while the second-hand ticked its way once around its circle, then with feverish impatience he tore the end from the envelope.

Benton's face paled a little as he drew out the many pages covered with a woman's handwriting, but there was no one to see that or to notice the tremor of his fingers.

For a moment he held the pages off, seeing only the "Dearest" at the top, and the wild way the pen had raced, forming almost shapeless characters.

"Dearest," she said in part, "I write now because I must turn to someone—because my heart must speak or break. All day I must smile as befits royalty, and act as befits one whose part is written for her. Unless there be an outlet, there must be madness. I have enclosed this envelope in another and enjoined you not to read it until March 5th. Then it will be too late for you to come to me. If you came to-night, you would find me hurrying out to meet you and to surrender. Duty would so gladly lay down its arms to Love, dear, and desert the fight.

"To-night I have slipped away from the uniforms, the tawdry mockery of a puppet court, to find the pitiful comfort of rehearsing my heart-ache to you, who own my heart. In my life here every hour is mapped, and I seem to move from cell to cell. So many obsequious jailers who call themselves courtiers stand about and seem to watch me, that I feel as if I had to ask permission to draw my breath. Out in the narrow streets of this little picture town, I see dark-skinned, bare-footed girls. Some of them carry skins of wine on their heads. All of them are poor. They also are gloriously free. As they pass the palace, they look up enviously, and I, from the inside, look out enviously. I know how Richard of the Lion Heart felt when he was a prisoner in France, only I have not the comfort of a Lion Heart, and it is not written in the book of things that you shall pass outside and hear my harp—and rescue me.... One little taste of liberty I give myself. It caused a terrible battle at first, but I was stubborn and told them that if I was going to be Queen I was going to do just what I wanted, and that if they didn't like it, they could get some other girl to be Queen, so of course they let me.... There is an old half-forgotten roadway walled in on both sides that runs through the town from this horrible palace to the woods upon the mountain. There is some sort of foolish legend that in the old days the Kings used to go by this protected road to a high point called Look-out Rock, and stand there where they could see pretty much all of this miserable little Kingdom and a great deal of the Mediterranean besides. No one uses it now except me; but I do as often as I can steal away. I dress in old clothes and take the little Inca god with me and no one knows us. We slip off among the bowlders and pine trees where the view is wonderful, and as his godship presides on a moss-covered rock and I sit on the carpet of pine needles, he gives me advice. Somewhere in these woods crowds of children live. They are very shy, and for a long time looked at me wonderingly from big liquid eyes, but now I have made friends with them and they come and sit around me in a circle and make me tell them fairy stories....

"Once, dear, I was strong enough to say 'no' to you. Twice I could not be."

The reader paused and scowled at the wall with set jaws.

"But when you read this, almost three thousand miles away, there will be only a few days between me and (it is hard to say it) the marriage and the coronation. He is to be crowned on the same day that we are married. Then I suppose I can't even write what is in my heart."

Benton rose and paced the narrow confines of the cabin. Suddenly he halted. "Even under sealed orders," he mused slowly, "one may dispose of three thousand miles. They, at least, are behind." A countenance somewhat drawn schooled its features into normal expressionlessness, as a few moments afterward he rose to open the door in response to a rapping outside.

As the door swung in a smile came to Benton's face: the first it had worn since that night when he had taken leave of Hope.

"You, Blanco!" he exclaimed. "Why, *hombre*, the anchor is scarce down. You are prompt!"

The physically superb man who stood at the threshold smiled. The gleam of perfect teeth accentuated the swarthy olive of his face and the crisp jet of his hair. His brown eyes twinkled good-humoredly. Jaw, neck and broad shoulders declared strength, while the slenderness of waist and thigh hinted of grace—a hint that every movement vindicated. It was the grace of the bull-fighter, to whom awkwardness would mean death.

"I had your letter. It was correctly directed—Manuel Blanco, *Calle Isaac Peral.*" The Spaniard smiled delightedly. "When one is once more to see an old friend, one does not delay. How am I? Ah, it is good of the *Señor* to ask. I do well. I have retired from the *Plaza de Toros*. I busy myself with guiding parties of *touristos* here and abroad—and in the collection and sale of antiques. But this time, what is your enterprise or pleasure, *Señor*? What do you in Spain?"

"My business in Spain," replied Benton slowly, "is to get out of Spain. After that I don't know. Will you go and take chances of anything that might befall? I sent for you to ask you whether you have leisure to accompany me on an enterprise which may involve danger. It's only fair to warn you."

Blanco laughed. "Who reads *mañana*?" he demanded, seating himself on the edge of the table, and busying his fingers with the deft rolling of a cigarette. "The *toreador* does not question the Prophets. I am at your disposition. But the streets of Cadiz await us. Let us talk of it all over the *table d'hôte*."

An hour later found the two in the *Calle Duke de Tetuan*, blazing with lights like a jeweler's show-case.

The narrow fissure between its walls was aflow with the evening current of promenaders, crowding its scant breadth, and sending up a medley of laughter and musical sibilants. Grandees strolled stiffly erect with long capes thrown back across their left shoulders to show the brave color of velvet linings. Young dandies of army and navy, conscious of their multi-colored uniforms, sifted along through the press, toying with rigidly-waxed mustaches and regarding the warm beauty of their countrywomen through keen, appreciative eyes, not untinged with sensuousness. Here and there a common *hombre* in short jacket, wide, low-crowned *sombrero* and red sash, zig-zagged through the pleasure-seekers to cut into a darker side street whence drifted pungent whiffs of garlic, black olives and peppers from the stalls of the street salad-venders. Occasionally a Moor in fez and wide-bagging trousers, passed silently through the volatile chatter, looking on with jet eyes and lips drawn down in an impervious dignity.

They found a table in one of the more prominent cafés from which they could view through the plate-glass front the parade in the street, as well as the groups of coffee-sippers within.

"Yonder," prompted Blanco, indicating with his eyes a near-by group, "he with the green-lined cape, is the Duke de Tavira, one of the richest men in Spain—it is on his estate that they breed the bulls for the rings of Cadiz and Seville. Yonder, quarreling over politics, are newspaper men and Republicans. Yonder, artists." He catalogued and assorted for the American the personalities about the place, presuming the curiosity which should be the tourist's attribute-in-chief.

"And at the large table—yonder under the potted palms, and half-screened by the plants—who are they?" questioned Benton perfunctorily. "They appear singularly engrossed in their talk."

"Assume to look the other way, *Señor*, so they will not suspect that we speak of them," cautioned the Andalusian. "I dare say that if one could overhear what they say, he could sell his news at his own price. Who knows but they may plan new colors for the map of Southern Europe?"

Benton's gaze wandered over to the table in question, then came uninquisitively back to Blanco's impassive face. It took more than European politics to distract him.

"International intrigue?" he inquired.

The eyes of the other were idly contemplating the street windows, and as he talked he did not turn them toward the men whom he described. Occasionally he looked at Benton and then vacantly back to the street parade, or the red end of his own cigarette.

"There is a small, and, in itself, an unimportant Kingdom with Mediterranean sea-front, called Galavia," said Blanco. Benton's start was slight, and his features if they gave a telltale wince at the word became instantly casual again in expression. But his interest was no longer forced by courtesy. It hung from that moment fixed on the narrative.

"Ah, I see the *Señor* knows of it," interpolated Blanco. "The tall man with the extremely pale face and the singularly piercing eye who sits facing us,"—Blanco paused,—"is the Duke Louis Delgado. He is the nephew of the late King of Galavia, and if—" the Spaniard gave an expressive shrug, and watched the smoke ring he had blown widen as it floated up toward the ceiling—"if by any chance, or mischance, Prince Karyl, who is to be crowned at Puntal three days hence, should be called to his reward in heaven, the gentleman who sits there would be crowned King of Galavia in his stead."

CHAPTER X

OF CERTAIN TRANSPIRINGS AT A CAFÉ TABLE

Benton's eyes seemed hypnotically drawn to the table pointed out, but he kept them tensely riveted on his coffee cup.

"Yes?" he impatiently prompted.

"Of course," continued Blanco absently, "no one could regret more profoundly than the Grand Duke any accident or fatality which might befall his royal kinsman, yet even the holy saints cannot prevent evil chances!" He paused to sip his coffee. "At the right of 'Louis, the Dreamer,' as he is called, sits the Count Borttorff, who is not greatly in favor with Prince Karyl. He, too, is a Galavian of noble birth, but Paris knows him better than Puntal. He on the left, the man with the puffed eyes and the dissipated mouth—you will notice also a scar over the left temple—" Blanco was regarding his cigarette tip as he flecked an ash to the floor—"is Monsieur Jusseret supposed to be high in the affairs of the French *Cabinet Noir*."

"There is one more—and a vacant chair," suggested Benton.

The *toreador* nodded. "True, I had not forgotten the other. Tall, black-haired, not unlike yourself in appearance, *Señor*, save for a heavier jaw and the mustache which points upward. He is an Englishman by birth, a native of the world by adoption. Once he bore a British army commission. Now he is seen in distinguished society"—Blanco laughed—"when distinguished society wants something done which clean men will not do. His name, just now, is Martin. In many quarters he is better known as the English Jackal. Where one sees him one may scent conspiracy."

In all the life and color compassed between the four walls of Moorish tiles and arches, Benton felt the magnet of the group irresistibly drawing his eyes to itself.

"And this gathering about a table for a cup of coffee, in Cadiz—what of it?" argued Benton. He tried to speak as if his curiosity were dilute and his thoughts west of the Atlantic. "Are they not all known here?"

Again Blanco gave the expressive Spanish shrug.

"Few people here know any of them. I only said, *Señor*, that if any chance should cause Galavia to mourn her new King that same chance would elevate the tall, pale gentleman from a café table to a throne. I did not say that the chance would occur."

"And yet?" urged Benton, his eyes narrowing, "your words seem to hint more than they express. What is it, Manuel?"

The Spaniard took a handful of matches from a porcelain receptacle on the table. He laid one down.

"Let that match," he smilingly suggested, "stand for the circumstance of the Grand Duke leaving Paris for Cadiz which is—well, nearer to Puntal—and less observant than Paris." He laid another on the marble table-top with its sulphur head close to the first, so that the two radiated from a common center like spokes from a hub. "Regard that as a coincidence of the arrival of the Count Borttorff from the other direction, but at the same time, and at the precise season of the coronation and marriage of the King." He looked at the two matches, then successively laid down others, all with the heads at the common center. "That," he said, "is the joining of the group by the distinguished Frenchman—that the presence of the English Jackal—that is the chance that runs against any King or Queen of meeting death. That—" he struck another match and held it a moment burning in his fingers "—regard that, *Señor*, as the flaring up of ambitions that are thwarted by a life or two."

He touched the burning match to the grouped tips of sulphur and his teeth gleamed white as he contemplated the little spurt of hissing flame. Then he dropped his flattened hand upon the tiny eruption and extinguished it, as his sudden grin died away to a bored smile.

HIS TEETH GLEAMED WHITE AS HE CONTEMPLATED THE LITTLE SPURT OF HISSING FLAME.

"There, it is over," he yawned, "and of course it may not happen. *Quien sabe?*"

"And if they should flare up—" Benton spoke slowly, carefully, "others might suffer than the King?"

"How should one say? The King alone would suffice, but Kings are rarely found in solitude," reasoned the Andalusian. "For a brief moment Europe looks with eyes of interest on the feasting little capital. The King will not be alone. No, it must be—so one would surmise—at the coronation."

"Good God!" Benton gaspingly breathed the exclamation. "But, man, think of it—the women—the children—the utterly innocent people—the Queen!"

The Spaniard leaned back, balancing his chair on two legs, his hands spread on the table. "*Si, Señor*, it is regrettable. Yet nothing on earth appears so easy to supply as Kings—except Queens. And after all, what is it to us—an American millionaire—a Cadiz *toreador*?"

For a moment Benton was silent. When he spoke it was in quick, clear-clipped interrogation.

"You know Puntal and Galavia?"

"As I know Spain."

"Manuel, suppose the quaking of a throne *does* interest me, you will go there with me—even though I may lead you where its fall may crush us both?"

The Spaniard grinned with a dazzling show of white teeth. His shoulders rose and fell in a shrug. "As well a tumbling castle wall as a charging bull."

"Good. The first thing is to learn all we can of Louis and his party."

"There is," observed Blanco calmly, "a table on this side also shielded by plants. From its angle we can observe,—and be ourselves protected from their view. However, we will first go for a stroll in the *calle* and return. The change of position will then be less noticeable. Also, the *Señor's* forehead is beaded with moisture. The air of the street will be grateful."

As Benton rose he noticed that the Grand Duke was leaning confidentially toward the member of the French *Cabinet Noir*.

Fifteen minutes later the two men were ensconced in their more sheltered coign, with wine glasses before them, and all the seeming of idle hours to kill.

"Is Louis ostensibly a friend of the throne?" demanded the American.

"Professedly, he is, *Señor*. He will write his felicitations when the marriage and the crowning occur—he will even send suitable gifts, but he will remain at his café here with his absinthe, or in Paris near the fair Comptessa Astaride, whom he adores, unless, of course, he goes to touch the match."

"Does he never return to Puntal?"

"Once in five years he has been there. Then he went quietly to his hunting lodge which is ten miles, as the crow flies from the capital, yet barred off by the mountain ridge. It is two days' journey by sea from Puntal, and save by the sea one comes only through the mountain pass, which is always guarded. Yet on that occasion heliographs reported his movements; the King's escort was doubled and the King went little abroad."

"Who stands at Louis' back? Revolutionists?"

"*Dios!* No, *Señor*. The Galavians are cattle. Karyl or Louis, it is one to them. Galavia is a key. The key cares not at what porter's belt it jingles. Europe cares who opens and closes the lock. *Comprende?* Spain cares, France cares, Italy cares, even the Northern nations care. The movement of pawns affects castles and kings."

Manuel suddenly halted in his flow of talk. "Blessed Saints!" he breathed softly. "When he comes nearer you will see him—the palms obscure him now. It is Colonel Von Ritz. He has just entered. He stands near Karyl and the throne. He is a great man wasted in a toy kingdom. All Europe envies the services which Von Ritz squanders on Galavia."

Benton looked up with a rush of memories, and was glad that the Galavian could not see him.

Like all the men concerned, Von Ritz was inconspicuously a civilian in dress, but as he came down the center of the room he was, as always, the commanding figure, challenging attention. His steady eyes swept the place with dispassionate scrutiny. His straight mouth-line betrayed no expression. He came slowly, idly, as though looking for someone. When still some distance from the table where sat the Duke Louis, he halted and their eyes met. Those of the Duke, as he inclined his head slightly, stiffly, wore a glint of veiled hostility. Those of Von Ritz, as he returned the salute, no whit more cordially, were blank, except that for the moment, as he stood regarding the party, his non-committal pupils seemed to bore into each face about the table and to catalogue them all in an insolent inventory.

Each man in the group uneasily shifted his eyes. Then Karyl's officer turned on his heel and left the place. Louis watched him, scowling, and as the Colonel passed into the street turned suddenly and spoke in a vehement whisper. Jusseret's sardonic lips twisted into a wry smile as though in recognition of an adversary's clever check.

The café was now filled. Few tables remained unoccupied, and of these, several were near that of the Ducal party.

Blanco rose. "Wait for me, *Señor*," he whispered, then went to the front of the café where Benton lost him in a crowd at the door. A moment later he came lurching back. His lower lip was stupidly pendent, his eyes heavy and dull, and as he floundered about he dropped with the aimless air of one heavily intoxicated into a chair by a vacant table not more than ten feet distant from that of Louis, the Dreamer.

There he remained huddled in apparent torpor and for some moments unobserved, until the Duke signaled to a passing waiter and indicated the *toreador* with a glance. The waiter came over to Blanco. "The *Señor* will find another table," he said with the ingratiating courtesy of one paying a compliment. "It is regrettable, but this one is reserved." Blanco appeared too stupid to understand, and when finally he did grasp the meaning he rose with profuse and clumsy apologies and staggered vacantly about in the immediate neighborhood of the conspiring coterie. Finally, after receiving further attention and guidance from the waiter, he returned to Benton, and dropping into his chair leaned over, his white teeth flashing a satisfied smile. "The matches may not flare, *Señor*," he said, "but it would appear it was planned. Now Martin and Borttorff cannot go to Puntal. Since the brief visit of Von Ritz they are branded men. The others are already known to Karyl's government."

Benton sat with his brows knitted intently listening.

"Now," went on Blanco, "there is one thing more. They await the man for whom they hold the empty chair."

There was a brief silence, then the Spaniard uttered a low exclamation of satisfaction. Benton glanced up to see a young man of frank face, blond mustache and Paris clothes drop into the vacant place with evident apologies for his tardiness.

"Ah," breathed Blanco again, "I feared it would be someone I did not know. He is the *Teniente* Lapas, of Karyl's Palace guard. The *pobrecito*! I wonder what post he hopes to adorn at the Court of the Pretender."

For a moment the Spaniard looked on with an expression of melancholy reflection. "That boy," he said "at last, has the trust and friendship of the King. Before him lies every prospect of advancement, yet he has been beguiled by the Countess Astaride, and throws himself into a plot against Karyl. It is pitiable when one is perfidious so young—and with such small cause."

"Who is the Countess Astaride?" inquired the American.

"One of the most beautiful women in Europe, to whom these children are playthings. For her there is only Louis Delgado. It is her firing of his dreams which makes him aspire to a throne. It is she who has the determination. He can see visions of power only in the colors of his absinthe glass. She uses men to her ends. Lapas is the latest—unless—" Blanco paused—"unless he is playing two parts, and really serves Karyl. Come, *Señor*, there is nothing further to interest us here."

CHAPTER XI

THE PASSING PRINCESS AND THE MISTAKEN COUNTESS

With the sapphire bay of Puntal at his back, his knees clasped between interlacing fingers, Benton sat on the stone sea-wall and affected to whistle up a lightness of heart. Near at hand sprawled a picturesque city, its houses tinted in pea-greens, pinks and soft blues, or as white and decorative as though fashioned in icing on a cake.

Clinging steeply to higher levels and leaning on buttressing walls, lay outspread vineyards and cane fields and gardens. Splotching the whole with imperial and gorgeous purple, hung masses of bougonvillea between trellis and masonry. At a more lofty line, where the sub-tropical profusion halted in the warning breath of a keener atmosphere, came the scrub growth and beyond that, in succeeding altitudes, the pine belt, the snow line and the film of trailing cloud on the white peaks.

Out of the center of the color-splashed town rose the square tower of the ancient cathedral, white in a coat of plaster for two-thirds of its height, but gray at its top in the nakedness of mossy stone.

To its dilapidated clock Benton's eyes traveled repeatedly and anxiously while he waited.

From the clock they wandered in turn to the road circling the bay, and the cliff at his left, where the jail-like walls of the King's Palace rose sheer from the rock, fifty feet above him.

From the direction of the Cathedral drifted fragments of band music, and the bugle calls of marching platoons. Everywhere festivity reigned, working great profits to the keepers of the wine-shops.

Manuel Blanco turned the corner and Benton slipped quickly down from his perch on the wall and fell into step as the other passed.

"It is difficult to learn anything, *Señor*." The Spaniard spoke low as he led the way outward from the city.

"Puntal is usually a quiet place and the festivities have made it like a child at a *fiesta*. One hears only 'Long live the King—the Queen!' There are to be illuminations to-night, and music, and the limit will be taken off the roulette wheels at the Strangers' Club. Bah! One could have read it in the papers without leaving Cadiz."

"Then you have learned nothing?"

"One thing, yes. An old friend of mine has come for the festivities from the Duke's estate. He says the pass is picketed and a guard is posted at the Look-out Rock."

"The Look-out Rock?" Benton repeated the words with an inflection of inquiry.

"Yes—look above you at the hill whose summit is less high than the ridge peaks—there below the snow." Blanco suddenly raised his voice from confidential undertone to the sing-song of the professional guide. "Yonder," he said, scarcely changing the direction of his pointed finger, "is the unfinished sanatorium for consumptives which the Germans undertook and left unfinished." Two soldiers were sauntering by, smart in newly issued uniforms of tall red caps, dark tunics, sky-blue breeches, and polished boots. "That point," went on Blanco, dropping his voice again, as they passed out of earshot, "is three thousand, five hundred feet above the sea. From the rock by the pines—if you had a strong glass, you could see the Galavian flag which flies there—the eye sweeps the sea for many empty leagues. One's gaze can also follow the gorge where runs the pass through the mountains. Also, to the other side, one has an eagle's glimpse of the Grand Duke's hunting lodge. There is an observatory just back of the rock and flag. The speck of light which you can see, like a splinter of crystal, is its dome, but only military astronomers now look through its telescope. There one can read the tale of open shutters or barred windows in the house of Louis, the Dreamer. You understand?"

"Yes."

"Now, do you see the thread of broken masonry zig-zagging upward from the Palace? That is a walled drive which runs part of the way up to the rock. In other days the Kings of Galavia went thus from their castle to the point whence they could see the peninsula spread out below like a map on the page of a school-book."

"Yes? What else?"

"This. The lodge of the Duke as seen by the telescope sleeps shuttered—an expanse of blank walls. Yet the Duke is there!"

"Louis—in Galavia?"

"Wait." Blanco laid his hand on the other's arm and smiled.

"My friend is superstitious—and ignorant. He tells how the Duke has a ship's mast with wires on a tower fronting the far side. He says Louis talks with the open sea."

"A Marconi mast?"

Manuel nodded.

Benton's eyes narrowed under drawn brows. When he spoke his voice was tense.

"In God's name, Manuel," he whispered, "what is the answer?"

The Spaniard met the gaze gravely. "I fancy, *Señor*," he said slowly, "the matches will burn."

"When? Where?"

"*Quien sabe?*" Blanco paused to light a cigarette. Two priests, their black robes relieved by crimson sashes and stockings, approached, and until they were at a safe distance he talked on once more at random with the sing-song patter of the guide. "That dungeon-like building is the old Fortress *do Freres*. It has clung to that gut of rock out there in the bay since the days when the Moors held the Mediterranean. It is said that the new King will convert it from a fortress into a prison. It is now employed as an arsenal."

Slowly the two men moved back to the busier part of the city. They walked in silence until they were swallowed in the crowds drifting near the Central Avenue. Finally Blanco leaned forward, moved by the anxious face of his companion. "*Mañana, Señor*," he suggested reassuringly. "Perhaps we may learn to-morrow."

"And to-morrow may be too late," replied Benton.

"Hardly, *Señor*. The marriage and coronation are the day following. It should be one of those occasions." Benton only shuddered.

They swung into the *Ruo Centrale*, between lining sycamores, olive trees and acacias, to be engulfed in a jostling press of feast-day humanity. Suddenly Benton felt his coat-sleeve tugged.

"Let us stop," Manuel shouted into his ear above the roar of the carnival clamor. "The Royal carriage comes."

Between a garden and the pavement ran a stone coping, topped by a tall iron grill, and laden with screening vines. The two men mounted this masonry and clung to the iron bars, as the crowd was driven back from the street by the outriders. Before Benton's eyes the whole mass of humanity swam in a blur of confusion and vertigo. The passing files of blue and red soldiery seemed wavering figures mounted on reeling horses. The King's carriage swung into view and a crescendo of cheering went up from the crowd.

Benton saw blurred circles of color whirling dizzily about a steady center, and the center was the slender woman at Karyl's side, who was the day after to-morrow to become his Queen. He saw the fixed smile with which she tried to acknowledge the salutations as the crowd eddied about her carriage. Her wide, stricken eyes were shimmery with imprisoned tears. To drive through the streets of Puntal with that half-stunned misery written clear in lips and eyes, she must, he knew, have reached the outmost border of endurance. Karyl bent solicitously forward and spoke, and she nodded as if answering in a dream, smiling wanly. It was all as some young Queen might have gone to the guillotine rather than to her coronation. As she looked bewilderedly from side to side her glance fell upon the clustering flowers of the vine. Benton gripped the iron bars and groaned, and then her eyes met his. For a moment her pupils dilated and one gloved hand convulsively tightened on the paneling of the carriage door. The man dropped into the crowd and was swallowed up, and he knew by her familiar gesture of brushing something away from her temples, that she believed she had seen an image projected from a troubled brain.

"Come," he said brokenly to his companion, "for God's sake get me out of this crowd."

The Strangers' Club of Puntal sits high on a solid wall of rock and overlooks the sea. Its beauty is too full of wizardry to seem real, and what nature had done in view and sub-tropical luxuriance the syndicate which operates the ball rooms, tea gardens, and roulette wheels has striven to abet. To-night a moon two-thirds full immersed the grounds in a bath of blue and silver, and far off below the cliff wall the Mediterranean was phosphorescent. In the room where the *croupiers* spun the wheels, the color scheme was profligate.

Benton idled at one of the tables, his eyes searching the crowd in the faint hope of discovering some thread which he might follow up to definite conclusion. Beyond the wheel, just at the *croupier's* elbow, stood a woman, audaciously yet charmingly gowned in red, with a scale-like shimmer of passementerie. A red rose in her black hair threw into conspicuous effect its intense luster.

She might have been the genius of *Rouge et Noir*. Her litheness had the panther's sinuous strength. The vivid contrast of olive cheeks, carmine lips and dark eyes, gave stress to her slender sensuousness.

Hers was the allurement of poppy and passion-flower. In her movements was suggestion of vital feminine force.

Perhaps the incurious glance of the American made itself felt, for as she threw down a fresh *louis d'or*, she looked up and their eyes met. For an instant her expression was almost that of one who stifles an impulse to recognize another. Possibly, thought Benton, she had mistaken him for someone else.

"*Mon dieu*," whispered a voice in French, "the Comptessa d'Astaride is charming this evening."

"Ah, such wit! Such charm!" enthused another voice at Benton's back. "She is most perfect in those gowns of unbroken lines, with a single rose." Evidently the men left the tables at once, for Benton heard no more. He also turned away a moment later to make way for an Italian in whose feverish eyes burned the roulette-lust. He went to the farthest end of the gardens, where there was deep shadow, and a seaward outlook over the cliff wall. There the glare of electric bulbs and blazing doorways was softened, and the orchestra's music was modulated. Presently he was startled by a ripple of laughter at his shoulder, low and rich in musical vibrance.

"Ah, it is not like this in your gray, fog-wrapped country."

Benton wheeled in astonishment to encounter the dazzling smile of the Countess Astaride. She was standing slender as a young girl, all agleam in the half-light as though she wore an armor of glowing copper and garnets.

"I beg your pardon," stammered the American, but she laid a hand lightly on his arm and smilingly shook her head.

"I know, Monsieur Martin, we have not met, but you were with the Duke at Cadiz. You have come in his interest. In his cause, I acknowledge no conventions." In her voice was the fusing of condescension and regal graciousness. "It was wise," she thoughtfully added, "to shave your mustache, but even so Von Ritz will know you. You cannot be too guarded."

For an instant Benton stood with his hands braced on the coping regarding her curiously. Evidently he stood on the verge of some revelation, but the rôle in which her palpable mistake cast him was one he must play all in the dark.

"You can trust me," she said with an impassioned note but without elevating her voice. "I am the Countess—"

"Astaride," finished Benton.

Then he cautiously added the inquiry: "Have you heard the plans that were discussed by the Duke, and Jusseret and Borttorff?"

"And yourself and Lieutenant Lapas," she augmented.

"And Lapas and myself," admitted Benton, lying fluently.

"I know only that Louis is to wait at his lodge to hear by wireless whether France and Italy will recognize his government," she hastily recited; "and that on that signal you and Lapas wait to strike the blow."

"Do you know when?" inquired the American, fencing warily in the effort to lead her into betrayal of more definite information.

"It must be soon—or never! But tell me, has Louis come? Has he reached his hunting lodge? Does he know that guards are at the rock? Do you, or Lapas, wait to flash the signal from the look-out? Ah, how my gaze shall be bent toward the flag-staff." Then, as her eyes wandered out to sea, her voice became soft with dreams. She laughed low and shook her head. "Louis, Louis!" she murmured. "When you are King! But tell me—" again she was anxious, executive, imperious—"tell me everything!"

Obviously he was mistaken for the English Jackal!

Benton countered anxiously. "Yet, Your Majesty,"—he bent low as he anticipated her ambition in bestowing the title—"Your Majesty asks so many questions all at once, and we may be interrupted."

Once more she was in a realm of air castles as she leaned on the stone coping and gazed off into the moonlight. "It is but the touching of a button," she murmured, "and *allons*! In the space of an explosion, dynasties change places." Suddenly she stood up. "You are right. We cannot talk here. I shall be missed. Take this"—she slipped a seal ring from her finger. "Come to me to-morrow morning. I am at the Hôtel de France. I shall be ostensibly out, but show the ring and you will be admitted. When I am Queen, you shall not go undecorated." She gave his hand a warm momentary pressure and was gone.

CHAPTER XII

BENTON MUST DECIDE

On the next afternoon at the base of the flag-staff above Look-out Rock, Lieutenant Lapas nervously swept the leagues of sea and land, spreading under him, with strong glasses. Though the air was somewhat rarer and cooler here than below, beads of sweat stood out on his forehead, and the cigarettes which he incessantly smoked followed each other with a furious haste which denoted mental unrest.

At a sound of foliage rustled aside and a displaced rock bumping down the slope, the watcher took the glasses from his eyes with a nervous start.

Up the hill from the left climbed an unknown man. His features were those of a Spaniard. As the officer's eyes challenged him he halted, panting, to mop his brow with the air of one who takes a breathing space after violent exertion. The newcomer smiled pleasantly as he leaned against a bowlder and genially volunteered: "It is a long journey from the shore." Then after a moment he added in a tone of respectful inquiry: "You are Lieutenant Lapas?"

The officer had regained his composure. He regarded the other with a mild scrutiny touched with superciliousness as he nodded acquiescence and in return demanded: "Who are you?"

"Do you see that speck of white down yonder by the sea?" Blanco drew close and his outstretched finger pointed a line to the Duke's lodge. "I come from there," he explained with concise directness.

The officer bit his lip.

"Why did you come?" The Spaniard paused to roll a cigarette before he answered:

"I come from the Duke, of course. Why else should I climb this accursed ladder of hills?"

"What Duke?" The interrogation tumbled too eagerly from the soldier's lips to be consonant with his wary assumption of innocence. "There are so many Dukes. Myself, I serve only the King."

The Spaniard's teeth gleamed, and there was a strangely disarming quality in the smile that broke in sudden illumination over his dark face.

"I have been here only a few days," explained Blanco. Then, lying with apt fluency, he continued: "I have arrived from Cadiz in the service of the Grand Duke Louis Delgado, who will soon be His Majesty, Louis of Galavia, and I am sent to you as the bearer of his message." He ignored the other's protestations of loyalty to the throne as completely as he ignored the frightened face of the man who made them.

Lapas had whitened to the lips and now stood hesitant. "I don't understand," he stammered.

The Spaniard's expression changed swiftly from good humor to the sternness of a taskmaster.

"The Duke is impatient," he asserted, "of delays and misunderstandings on the part of his servants. His Grace believed that your memory had been well schooled. Louis, the King, may prove forgetful of those who are forgetful of Louis, the Duke."

Lapas still stood silent, pitiably unnerved. If the man was Karyl's spy an incautious reply might cost him his life. If he was genuinely a messenger from the Pretender any hesitation might prove equally fatal.

Time was important. Blanco drew from his pocket a gold seal ring which until last night had adorned the finger of the Countess Astaride. Upon its shield was the crest of the House of Delgado. At the sight of the familiar quarterings, the officer's face became contrite, apologetic, but above all immeasurably relieved.

"Caution is so necessary," he explained. "One cannot be too careful. It is not for myself alone, but for the Duke also that I must have a care."

Blanco accepted the explanation with a bow, then he spoke energetically and rapidly, pressing his advantage before the other's weakness should lead him into fresh vacillation.

"The Duke feared that there might be some misunderstanding as to the signal and the programme. He wished me to make it clear to you."

Lapas nodded and, turning, led the way through the pine trees to a small kiosk that was something between a sentinel box and a signal station built against the walls of the old observatory.

"I think I understand," said Lapas, "but I shall be glad to have you repeat the Duke's commands and inform me if any changes have been made."

"No, the arrangements stand unaltered," replied the Spaniard. "My directions were that you should repeat to me the order of your instructions and that I should judge for His Grace whether or not your memory is retentive. There must be no hitch."

"I don't know you," demurred Lapas.

"His Grace knows me—and trusts me. That should be sufficient," retorted Blanco. "I bring you credentials which you will refuse to recognize at your own risk. Unless I were in the confidence of the Duke, I could scarcely be here with a knowledge of your plans."

Blanco's eyes blazed in sudden and well simulated wrath. "I have no time to waste in argument. Choose quickly. Shall I return to Louis and inform him that you refuse to trust those he selects to bear his orders?"

For an instant the Spaniard stood contemptuously regarding the other's terror, then with a disgusted exclamation he turned on his heel and started to the door of the kiosk. But Lapas was in a moment catching at his elbow and protesting himself convinced. He led Blanco back to a seat.

"Listen." The Lieutenant sat at the crude table in the center of the small room and talked rapidly, as one rehearsing a well-learned lesson.

"The Fortress *do Freres* is stocked with explosives. Karyl goes there with Von Ritz and others of his suite to inspect the place with the view of turning it into a prison. The Grand Duke, waiting at his hunting lodge, is to receive by wireless the message from Jusseret and Borttorff, who convey the verdict of Europe, as to whether or not it is decided to recognize his Government. If their message be favorable, he will raise the Galavian flag on the west tower of the hunting lodge, and I shall relay the message here with the flag at Look-out Point. This flag-pole will be the signal to those in the city whose fingers are on the key, and whose key will explode the powder in *do Freres.* If the flag which now flies from the flag-staff here is still flying when the King enters the fortress, the cap will explode. If the flag-staff is empty, the King's visit will be uneventful. It will require fifteen minutes for the King to go from the Palace to the Fortress. I must not remain here—I must be where I can see."

Lapas rose and consulted his watch with nervous haste. "You will excuse me?" he added. "I must be at my post. Are you satisfied?"

Blanco also rose, bowing as he drew back the heavy chair he had occupied. "I am quite satisfied," he approved. His hands were gripping the chairback and when Lapas had taken two paces to the front, and Blanco had appraised the distance between, the chair left the floor. With the same lightning swiftness of motion that had brought salvos of applause from the bull-rings of Cadiz and Seville, he swung it above his head and brought down its cumbersome weight in an arc.

Lapas, his eyes fixed on the door, had no hint. A picture of serene sky and steady mountains was blotted from his brain. There was blackness instead—and unconsciousness.

A bleeding scalp told the *toreador* that the blow had only cut and stunned.

Rapidly he bound and gagged his captive. Dragging him back through the narrow room he made certainty doubly sure by tying him to the base of the neglected telescope in the abandoned observatory.

A hundred yards below the rock, tucked out of sight of the man at the flag-pole, stretched a ledge-like strip of level ground, backed by the thick tangle of growth which masked the slope. Beyond its edge of roughly blocked and crevassed stone, the gorge fell away a dizzy thousand feet. Out of the pines struggled the half-overgrown path where once a road had led from the castle. This way the earlier Lords of Galavia had come to look across the backbone of the peninsula, to the east.

As Benton paced the ledge impatiently, awaiting the outcome of Blanco's reconnoiter, he noticed with a nauseating sense of onrushing peril how the purpled shadows of the mountains were lengthening across the valley and beginning to creep up the other side.

Each time his pacing brought him to the edge of the clearing he paused to look down at the sullen walls of Karyl's castle.

A woman, flushed and breathless from the climb, pushed through the scrub pines at the path's end and stopped suddenly at the marge of the clearing. Her slender girlish figure, clad in corduroy skirt and blue jersey, was poised with lance-like straightness, and a grace as free as a boy's. Her hands, cased in battered gauntlets, went suddenly to her breast, as though she would muffle the palpitant heart beneath the jersey. She stood for a moment looking at the man and the ultramarine of her eyes clouded slowly into gray. The pink flush of exercise died instantly to pallor in her cheeks.

Then the lips overcame an impulse to quiver and spoke slowly in an undertone and with marked effort. "This is twice that I have seen you," she whispered, "although you are three thousand miles away."

The man wheeled, not suddenly, but heavily and slowly. "I am real," he answered simply.

Cara put out one hand like a sleep-walker, and came forward, still incredulous.

"Cara, dearest one!" he said impetuously. "You must have known that I would be near you—that I would be standing by, even though I couldn't help!"

She shook her head. "I have been having these hallucinations, you know, of late." She explained as though to herself. "I guess it's—it's just missing people so that does it."

She was close to him now, close, too, to the sheer drop of the cliff, walking forward with eyes wide and fixed on his face. He took a quick step forward and swept her to him, crushing her against his breast.

She gave a glad exclamation of realization, and her own arms closed impulsively around his neck.

"You are real! You are real!" she whispered, looking into his eyes, her gauntleted hands holding his face between them.

"Cara," he begged, "listen to me. It's my last plea. You said in the letter I have in my pocket—there where your heart is beating—that you could not refuse me if I came again. Dear, this is 'again.' The *Isis* is a speck out there at sea awaiting a signal. Will you go? I have no throne to offer, but—"

"Don't," she cried, holding a hand over his lips. "For a minute—just for a little golden minute—let us forget thrones." Then as the furrow came back between her brows: "Oh, boy, it's my destiny to be always strong enough to resist happiness when I might have it by being less strong, and always too weak to bear bravely what must be borne—when it can't be helped."

He stood silent.

After a moment she went on. "And I love you. Ah, you know that well enough, but up there beyond your head which I love, I see the green and white and blue flag of Galavia which I hate, and destiny commands me to be disloyal to you for loyalty to it. On the eve of life imprisonment," she went on, clinging to him, "I have stolen away to play truant perhaps for the last time—still craving freedom, longing for you; and now I find freedom, and you, just to lose you again! I can't—I can't—yes—I can—I will!"

Suddenly he held her off at arms' length and looked at her with a strange wide-eyed expression of discovery.

"But," he cried with the vehemence of a sudden thought, "you are up here—safe! Safe, whatever happens down there! Nothing that occurs there can affect you!"

"Safe, of course," she spoke wonderingly. "What danger is there?"

The man turned. "For God's sake—let me think a moment!" He dropped on the pine needles and sat with his hands covering his face and his fingers pressed into his temples. She came over.

"Does that prevent your thinking?" she softly asked, dropping on her knees at his side and letting one hand rest on his shoulder.

For moments, lengthening into minutes, he sat immovable, fighting back the agonized and torrential flood of thought which burst upon him with unwarned temptation. The danger was not after all a danger to the woman he loved, but a menace to his enemy. She was safe three thousand feet above the threatening city. He had only to hold his hand, perhaps, for a half-hour; had only to keep her here and let matters follow their course.

He was not entertaining the thought, except to assure himself that he could not entertain it, but it was racking him with its suddenness. The King was there—in peril. She was here—safe. Insistently these two facts assaulted his brain.

"Pardon, *Señor.*" Blanco broke noisily down through the pines and halted where the path emerged. For an instant he stood in bewildered surprise.

"Pardon, Your Highness—" he exclaimed, bending low; then, quenching the recognition in his eyes and assuming mistake, he laughed. "Ah, I ask forgiveness, *Señorita.* I mistook you for the Princess. The resemblance is strong. I see my error."

"Manuel!" Benton rose unsteadily and stared at the *toreador* with a face pallid as chalk. He spoke wildly, "Quick, Manuel—have you learned anything?"

The Spaniard glanced inquiringly at the girl, and as Benton nodded reassurance went on in a lowered voice. Only fragments of his speech reached Cara's ears. Her own thoughts left her too apathetic to listen.

"The plan is this. It is to happen at the Fortress *do Freres* this afternoon while the King inspects the arsenal. Now, in fifteen minutes!" He pointed down toward the city. "See, the cortége leaves the Palace! Lapas was to be here at the rock—the blessed Saints help him! He is hobbled to his telescope." Swiftly he rehearsed the story as it had come from the lips of Lapas.

Benton was studying the Duke's lodge with his glasses. "There is a flag flying on the west tower," he muttered.

He turned slowly toward the Princess. Outstanding veins were tracing cordlike lines on his temples. His fingers trembled as he focused the glasses.

Blanco looked slowly from one to the other. Suddenly he threw back both shoulders and his eyes grew bright in full comprehension of the situation he had discovered.

"*Señor!*" he whispered.

"Yes?" echoed the American in a dull voice.

"*Señor*—suppose—suppose I have confused the signals?" The tone was insinuating.

Benton's mind flashed back to a Sunday School class of his childhood and his infantile horror for the tale of a tempter on a high mountain offering the possession of all the world if only—if only—

He took a step forward. Speech seemed to choke him.

"In God's name!" he cried, "you have not forgotten?"

The Spaniard slowly shook his head and smiled. The expression gave to his face a touch of the sinister. "No—but it is yet possible to forget, *Señor.* I serve no King, I serve you. Sometimes a mistake is the truest accuracy. *Quien sabe?*"

The Andalusian looked at the girl who stood puzzled and waiting. "Sometimes in the *Plaza de Toros, Señor,*" he went on, speaking rapidly and tensely, "the throngs cry, '*Bravo, matador!*' and toss coins into the ring. Yet in a moment the same throngs may shout until their throats are hoarse: '*Bravo, toro!*' A King is like a bull in the ring, *Señor*—he has a fickle fate. To me he is nothing—if it pleases them—it is their King—let them do as they wish." He shrugged his shoulders.

Benton straightened. "Manuel," he said with a strained tone, "the flag comes down."

The Andalusian smiled regretfully, and once more shrugged his shoulders.

"As you say, *Señor,* but are you sure you wish it so?"

"Manuel, I mean that!" said the American with a steadied voice. "And for God's sake, Manuel," he added wildly, "throw the rope over the gorge when you have done it!"

For a moment Benton stood rigid, his hands clenched together at his back as he watched the quick step of the Andalusian climbing to the flag-staff. At last he turned dully and looked down where he could see the royal cortége, not yet half-way along the road to the fortress, then he went over to the girl's side.

"Cara," he said, "I have earned the right to kiss you good-by."

"It's yours without the earning, but good-by—!" She shuddered. "What does it all mean?" she asked in bewilderment. "What was it you discussed?"

"Listen," he commanded. "Tell Von Ritz or Karyl that Lapas is a traitor and a prisoner in the observatory; that Louis is at his lodge and that the

Countess Astaride is a conspirator in a plot to assassinate the King. Tell them that a percussion cap and key connect the magazines of *do Freres* with the city."

The Princess looked at him with eyes that slowly widened in amazed comprehension. "I understand," she whispered. "And the flag—see, it is coming down—that means?"

He dropped on one knee and lifted her fingers to his lips. "It means that you are to be crowned Queen in Galavia to-morrow," he answered with a groan. "Long live the Queen!"

CHAPTER XIII

CONCERNING FAREWELLS AND WARNINGS

"To-morrow!" repeated the girl with a shudder.

Both stood silent under such a strain as cannot be long sustained. At the crunch of branch underfoot and the returning Blanco's, "*Señor! Señor!*" both started violently.

"Look, *Señor*," exclaimed the Spaniard. "The King has entered the fortress." Then, seeing that the eyes of both man and girl turned at his words from an intent gaze, not on the town but the opposite hills, he added, half-apologetic: "I shall go, *Señor*, and look to my prisoner. If you need me, I shall be there."

With the same stricken misery in her eyes that they had worn as she passed in her carriage, Cara remained motionless and silent.

The bottom of the valley grew cloudy with shadow. The sun was kissing into rosy pink the snow caps of the western ridge. A cavalcade of horsemen emerged at last from *do Freres* and started at a smart trot for the Palace. Cara pointed downward with one tremulous finger. Benton nodded.

"Safe," he said, but without enthusiasm.

"I must go." Cara started down the path and the man walked beside her as far as the battered gate which hung awry from its broken columns. Over it now clambered masses of vine richly purple with bougonvillea. She broke off a branch and handed it to him. "Purple," she said again, "is the color of mourning and royalty."

Blanco noted the coming of evening and realized that it would be well to reach the level of the city before dark. He knew that if Lapas was to be turned over to Karyl's authorities, steps to that end should be taken before he was discovered and released by those of his own faction. He accordingly made his way back to the gate.

Benton was still standing, looking down the alley-way which ran between the half ruined lines of masonry. His shoulders unconsciously sagged.

The Spaniard approached quietly and stood for a moment unwilling to interrupt, then in a low voice touched with that affectionate note which men are not ashamed to show even to other men in the Latin countries, he said: "*Señor* Benton!"

The American turned and put out his hand, grasping that of the *toreador*. His grip said what his lips left unworded.

"*Dios mio!*" exclaimed Blanco with a black scowl. "We saved the King, but we bought his life and his throne too high! He cost too dear!"

"Blanco," Benton spoke with difficulty, "I have brought you with me and you have asked no questions. The story is not mine to tell."

The Andalusian raised a hand in protestation.

"It is not necessary that you tell me anything, *Señor*. I have seen enough. And I know the King was not worth the price."

Benton shook his head. "Are you going on with me, now that you know what you know?"

"*Señor*, it grieves me that you should ask. I told you I was at your disposition." The Spaniard went on talking rapidly, talking with lips and eyes and gesture. "When you came to Cadiz and took me with you on the small steamer, I did not ask why. I thought it was as Americans are interested in all things—or perhaps because the many million *pesetas* of the *Señor's* fortune might be affected by changing the map of Europe. No matter. You were interested. It was enough."

He swept both hands apart.

"But had I known then what to-day has taught me, I should have held my tongue that evening when the Pretender plotted in the café."

"To-morrow," said Benton slowly, "there will be festivity. I can't be here then. I must leave to-night—but you, *amigo mio*, you must stay and watch. If Lapas is taken prisoner and silenced there will be no one in Puntal who will suspect you. No one knew me and if I leave at once, the Countess will hardly learn who was the mysterious man to whom she gave a ring."

"But, *Señor*,"—Blanco was dubious—"would it not be better that I should be with you?"

"You can serve me better by remaining here. I would rather have you near Her."

The man from Cadiz nodded and crossed himself.

"I am pledged, *Señor*," he asserted.

"Then," continued the American, "for a time we must separate. The *Isis* will sail to-night."

The men walked together to the terminal station of the small ratchet railway. When they parted the Spaniard and the yachtsman had arranged a telegraph code which might be used by the small but complete wireless equipment of the *Isis*. An hour later the launch from the yacht took him aboard at the ancient stone jetty, where the fruit-venders and wine-sellers shouted their jargon, and the seaweed clung to the landing stage.

When Karyl had returned to the Palace after the inspection of the Fortress *do Freres*, he had sent word at once to that part of the Palace where Cara had her suite. She was accompanied by her aunt, the Duchess of Apsberg, and her English cousin, Lilian Carrowes, who also knew something of the life in America with the Bristows.

The King craved an interview. He had not seen her since morning and his request conveyed the desolation occasioned by the long interval of empty time.

The girl, who in the more informal phases had consistently defied the Court etiquette, sent an affirmative reply, and Karyl, still in uniform and dust-stained, came at once to the rooms where she was to receive him.

There was much to talk of, and the King came forward eagerly, but the girl halted his protestations and rapidly sketched for him the summary of all she had learned that afternoon.

With growing astonishment Karyl listened, then slowly his brows came together in a frown.

It was distasteful to him beyond expression to feel that he owed his life and throne to Benton, but of that he said nothing. Lapas had been, in the days of his childhood, his playmate. He had been the recipient of every possible favor, and Karyl, himself ingenuous and loyal to his friends, felt with double bitterness that not only had his enemy saved him, but, too, his friend had betrayed him.

Then came a hurried message from Von Ritz, who begged to see the King at once. The soldier must have been only a step behind his messenger, for hardly had his admittance been ordered when he appeared.

The officer looked from the King to the Princess, and his eyes telegraphed a request for a moment of private audience.

"You may as well speak here," said Karyl dryly. "Her Highness knows what you are about to say."

"Lieutenant Lapas," began Von Ritz imperturbably, "has not been seen at the Palace to-day. His duties required his presence this evening. He was to be near Your Majesty at the coronation to-morrow."

"Where is he?" demanded the King.

"That is what I should like to know," replied Von Ritz. "I learn that last night the Count Borttorff was in Puntal and that Lapas was with him. To-day the Countess Astaride left Puntal, greatly agitated. I am informed that from her window she watched *do Freres* with glasses during Your Majesty's visit there, and that when you left she swooned. Within ten minutes she was on her way to the quay and boarded the out-going steamer for Villefranche. These things may spell grave danger."

So rarely had Karyl been able to anticipate Von Ritz in even the smallest matter that now, despite his own chagrin, he could not repress a cynical smile as he inquired: "What do you make of it?"

Von Ritz shook his head. "I shall report to Your Majesty within an hour," he responded.

"That is not necessary," Karyl spoke coolly. "You will, I am informed, find Lieutenant Lapas bound to a telescope at the Rock. You will find the explosives at *do Freres* connected with a percussion cap which was to have been touched while we were there this afternoon. The Countess was disappointed because the percussion cap was not exploded. Sometimes, when ladies are bitterly grieved, they swoon."

For a moment the older man studied the younger with an expression of surprise, then the sphinx-like gravity returned to his face.

"Your Majesty, may I inquire why the cap failed to explode?" he asked, with pardonable curiosity.

"Because"—Karyl's cheeks flushed hotly—"an American gentleman, who had been here a few hours, intercepted the signal—and reversed it."

For an instant Von Ritz looked fixedly into the face of the King, then he bowed.

"In that case," he commented, "there are various things to be done."

CHAPTER XIV

COUNTESS AND CABINET NOIR JOIN FORCES

When Monsieur François Jusseret, the cleverest unattached ambassador of France's *Cabinet Noir*, had first met the Countess Astaride, his sardonic eyes had twinkled dry appreciation.

This meeting had seemed to be the result of a chance introduction. It had in reality been carefully designed by the French manipulator of underground wires. Louis Delgado he already knew, and held in contempt, yet Louis was the only possible instrument for use in converting certain vague possibilities into definite realities. Changing the nebulous into the concrete; shifting the dotted line of a frontier from here to there on a map; changing the likeness that adorned a coin or postage-stamp: these were things to which Monsieur Jusseret lent himself with the same zest that actuates the hunting dog and makes his work also his passion.

If the vacillation of Louis Delgado could be complemented by the strong ambition of a woman, perhaps he might be almost as serviceable as though the strength were inherent. And Paris knew that Louis worshiped at the shrine of the Countess Astaride. The Countess was therefore worth inspecting.

The presentation occurred in Paris, when the Duke took his acquaintance to the charming apartments overlooking the Arc de Triomphe, where the lady poured tea for a small *salon* enlisted from that colony of ambitious and broken-hearted men and women who hold fanatically to the faith that some throne, occupied by another, should be their own. Here with ceremony and stately etiquette foregathered Carlists and Bonapartists and exiled Dictators from South America. Here one heard the gossip of large conspiracies that come to nothing; of revolutions that go no farther than talk.

In Paris the Duke Louis Delgado was nursing, with lukewarm indignation, wrath against his royal uncle of Galavia who had fixed upon him a sort of modified exile.

Louis had only a languid interest in the feud between his arm of the family and the reigning branch. He would willingly enough have taken a scepter from the hand of any King-maker who proffered it, but he would certainly never, of his own incentive, have struck a blow for a throne.

Sometimes, indeed, as he sat at a café table on the *Champs Elysées* when awakening dreams of Spring were in the air and a military band was playing in the distance, dormant ambitions awoke. Sometimes when he watched the opalescent gleam in his glass as the garçon carefully dripped water over absinthe, he would picture himself wresting from the incumbent, the Crown of Galavia, and would hear throngs shouting "Long live King Louis!" At such moments his stimulated spirit would indulge in large visions, and his half-degenerate face would smile through its gentle but dissipated languor.

Louis Delgado was a man of inaction. He had that quality of personal daring which is not akin to moral resoluteness. He was ready enough at a fancied insult to exchange cards and meet his adversary on the field, but a throne against which he plotted was as safe, unless threatened by outside influences, as a throne may ever be.

When Louis presented Jusseret to the Countess Astaride there flashed between the woman of audacious imagination and the master of intrigue a message of kinship. The Frenchman bent low over her hand.

"That hand, Madame," he had whispered, "was made to wield a scepter."

The Countess had laughed with the melodious zylophone note that caressed the ear, and had flashed on Jusseret her smile which was a magic thing of ivory and flesh and sudden sunshine. She had held up the slender fingers of the hand he had flattered, possibly a trace pleased with the effect of the Duke's latest gift, a huge emerald set about with small but remarkably pure brilliants. She had contemplated it, critically, and after a brief silence had let her eyes wander from its jewels to the Frenchman's face.

"Wielding a scepter, Monsieur," she had suggested smilingly, "is less difficult than seizing a scepter. I fear I should need a stronger hand."

"Ah, but Madame," the Frenchman had hastened to protest, "these are the days of the deft finger and the deft brain. Even crowns to-day are not won in tug-of-war."

The woman had looked at him half-seriously, half-challengingly.

"I am told, Monsieur Jusseret," she said, "that no government in Europe has a secret which you do not know. I am told that you have changed a crown or two from head to head in your career. Let me see *your* hand."

Instantly he had held it out. The fastidiously manicured fingers were as tapering and white as her own.

"Madame," he observed gravely, "you flatter me. My hand has done nothing. But I do not attribute its failure to its lack of brawn."

"Some day," murmured Delgado, from his inert posture in the deep cushions of a divan, "when the time is ripe, I shall strike a decisive blow for the Throne of Galavia."

Jusseret's lip had half-curled, then swiftly he had turned and flashed a look of inquiry upon the woman. Her eyes had been on Louis and she had not caught the quick glint that came into the Frenchman's pupils, or the thoughtful regard with which he studied her and the Duke across the edge of his teacup. Later, when he rose to make his adieux, she noted the thoughtful expression on his face.

"Sometimes," he had said enigmatically, and had paused to allow his meaning to sink in, "sometimes a scepter stays where it is, not because the hand that holds it is strong, but because the outstretched hand is weak or inept. Your hand is suited."

She had searched his eyes with her own just long enough to make him feel that in the give-and-take of glances hers did not drop or evade, and he, trained in the niceties of diplomatic warfare, had caught the message.

So the Countess had been fired with ardent dreams and later, when the time seemed ripe, it was to her that Jusseret went, and with her that he made his secret alliance.

The ambitions cherished by Marie Astaride to become Louis' queen were secondary to a sincere devotion for Louis himself.

When at the last he had weakened and threatened to crumple, it was she who goaded him back to resolution. When the Duke had gone half-heartedly to his lodge to await the decision of the European Powers, it was she who went to Puntal to direct the conspirators and watch, from the windows of her hotel suite, the fortress on the jetty.

Her one deplorable error had been in mistaking Benton for Martin. This had been natural enough. Though she had never met the "English Jackal," she had once or twice seen him at a distance, and she had been misled by a strong resemblance and an excessive eagerness.

The afternoon she had spent on the balcony of her suite, her eyes fixed on the Fortress *do Freres*.

At last, with a wildly beating heart she had seen the King, Von Ritz and the escort ride up to the entrance and disappear. She had waited—waited—waited, her nerves set for the climax, until the continued silence seemed an unendurable shock.

Then the King and escort emerged. She, sitting pale and rigid, saw them mount and turn back unharmed toward the city. Her ears, eagerly set for the detonation which should shake the town and reverberate along the mountain sides, ached with the emptiness of silence.

Across the street a soldier, off duty and in civilian clothes, sat on the sea-wall and whittled. Incidentally he noticed that Madame the Countess was interested beyond the usual in some matter. He was there to notice Madame the Countess. His instructions from Von Ritz had been to keep a record of her goings and comings, and who came to see her or went away.

Therefore, when the King and his small retinue had trotted past the window and when Madame the Countess rose to go in, and when just as she crossed the low sill of the window she suddenly caught up both hands to her throat and fell heavily to the floor, the soldier, whittling a small crucifix, made a record of that also. When a moment later a gentleman whom he had not seen in Puntal for months, but whom he knew as the Count Borttorff, because that gentleman had formerly been Major of his battalion, hurriedly left a closed carriage and entered the place, the incident was noted. When still later both Borttorff and the Countess emerged and reëntered the conveyance, driving rapidly away, he likewise noted these things. Going from the pier whither he had followed the closed carriage, he reported his observations with soldierly dispatch to Colonel Von Ritz.

The Grand Duke Louis meanwhile, waiting in great anxiety, had received the message which had come by the wireless mast. The words were in code, and being translated they read: "France, Italy, Spain, Portugal will recognize. Strike." The signature was "Jt.," which Delgado knew for Jusseret. The Duke had been greatly excited. He paced the room in a nervous tremor. It was arranged that a small steamer, which had stood a short distance offshore since yesterday to relay the wireless message and make it doubly sure, should pick the Duke up as soon as Lapas signaled by a triple dip of the flag that the fortress had been destroyed. The steamer was then to rush the Grand Duke around the cape to Puntal, bringing him in as though he had come from Spain. Those conspirators who were in the capital, strengthened by those who would declare for Louis, with Karyl dead and no other heir existent, would proclaim him King. Lapas would see that the royal salute was fired as the steamer entered the harbor, and the Countess would either meet him and explain all the details or would speak with him by Marconi if she had left the town.

Louis spent the forenoon in an agony of anxiety and impatience. All afternoon he watched through binoculars the white and blue and green flag on the rock above him. He was waiting for the triple dip that should tell him the fortress had been scattered in débris and with it the government. Evidently the King was late going to the arsenal.

He had imagined it would be earlier. The hours dragged interminably. Louis walked the stone buttress where the flag which he had raised in signal to Lapas flapped and whipped against its staff. At last his binoculars, fixed on the rock, caught the dip of the colors there. With a great sigh of relief the Duke watched to see them rise and dip, rise and dip again. The flag came down the length of the pole—and did not go up.

Panic seized the Pretender. There was no way of talking with the ridge three thousand feet above. It was a climb of an hour and a half by the pass. Evidently there had been a miscarriage. In the prearranged code of flag signals the only provision for the drooping of the colors on the hill was in the event that it should be wished to stop the explosion. That would be only in the event of refusal by the governments to recognize; the governments had not refused! Possibly Lapas had turned traitor!

There had also been some unexplained delay seaward. The little steamer, which should have remained near by, was a speck on the horizon, and without her there was no possibility of escape. Wildly Louis, the Dreamer, hurried to his improvised Marconi station and called the ship. Finally toward evening came a response and with it a message from somewhere out at sea, relayed from ship to ship around the peninsula.

The message said simply in code: "Failure. Make your escape." It was signed "M. A."—Marie Astaride.

Louis rushed, panic-stricken, down to the shore. He and the few men with him paced the beach in the settling twilight with desperate anxiety. The steamer seemed to creep in, snail-like, over the smooth water. Meanwhile binoculars fixed on the pass showed a number of small specks sifting like ants through the lofty opening. Troops were advancing. It was now the life-and-death question of which would arrive first, the boats from the ship that had stood off at sea a bit too long, or the soldiers coming across the broken backbone of the mountains.

At last the ship had drawn near, and circled under full steam far enough out to get away to a flying start as soon as the Ducal party had been taken on board. Small boats were rushed toward the beach and Louis, the Dreamer, with his party waded knee-deep into the water to meet the rescuers.

At the same moment a bugle call announced the coming of Karyl's soldiery.

As Louis Delgado went over the side, he turned quickly back and, leaning over the rail, gazed through the settling darkness toward shore.

"Do we make for Puntal, Your Majesty?" inquired the captain, saluting.

Louis turned coldly. "No."

The officer looked at the Duke for a moment and read defeat in his eyes.

"Where then—Your Grace?" he inquired.

Louis winced under the quick amendment of title. "Anywhere," he said shortly; "anywhere—except Puntal."

CHAPTER XV

THE TOREADOR BECOMES AMBASSADOR

Manuel Blanco was ubiquitous during the first days following the coronation. He listened to the fragments of talk that drifted along the streets. He frequented the band concerts in the Public Gardens and drank native vintages in the wine-shops. He elbowed his way naïvely into chattering groups with his ears primed for a careless word. Nowhere did he catch a note hinting of intrigue or danger. It seemed a sound conclusion that if the plotters had not entirely surrendered their project for switching Kings in Galavia, their conspiracies were being once more fomented on foreign soil, just as the first plan had been incubated in Cadiz.

One evening shortly after the dual celebration, a steamer laden with tourists lay at anchor in the bay, outlined in points of light like a set-piece of fireworks. Hundreds of new sight-seeing faces swarmed along the narrow, cobbled streets. This would be a great night in the Strangers' Club and Blanco decided to spend an hour there.

In evening dress he moved through the gardens and pavilions of the casino on the rock, where with the coming of darkness the gayety of the town began to focus and sparkle.

The coronation of Karyl had brought to an end official mourning for the late King, and the crêpe which had palled the national insignia on all public buildings had been cleared away. With this restoration of public gayety came a liberal sprinkling of uniforms to the throngs that crowded the ball-rooms, tea-gardens and gambling halls.

Blanco was standing apart, looking on, when he felt a light touch on his shoulder and turned to find a young officer at his back who smilingly begged him for a moment in the gardens. The Spaniard noticed that the man who addressed him wore the epaulettes of a Captain of Infantry and the added stripe and crown of gold lace at the cuff which designated service in the household of the reigning family.

He turned and accompanied the officer through the wide door into the lantern-hung grounds, passing between the groups which clustered everywhere about small wicker tea-tables. There were no quiet or secluded spots in the gardens of the Strangers' Club to-night, but after a brief glance right and left the Captain led the way to a table in a shadowed niche between two doors. The light there was more shadowed and the tides of promenaders did not crowd so close upon it as elsewhere. As the two came up a third man rose from this table and Manuel found himself looking into the flinty eyes of Colonel Von Ritz.

Von Ritz spoke briefly. If *Señor* Blanco could spare the time, His Majesty wished to speak with him.

The younger officer turned back into the casino and Von Ritz led the *toreador* through the front gardens, where the tennis courts lay bare between the palms. The acacias and sycamores were soft, dark spots against the far-flung procession of the stars.

The street outside was crowded with fiacres and cabs. Von Ritz signaled to a footman and in a moment more Blanco and his escort had stepped into a closed carriage and were being driven toward the Palace. They entered by a side passage and the Colonel conducted him through several halls and chambers filled with uniformed officers, and finally into a more remote part of the building where they met only an occasional servant. At last they came into a great room entirely empty but for themselves. About the walls hung ripened portraits. The decorations were of Arabesque mosaics with fantastic panels of Moorish tiling. It might have been a grandee's house in Seville, patterned on the Alcazar. Evidently this was part of a private suite. Heavy portières were only partly drawn across a wide window with the sill at the floor level, and through them Blanco dimly saw a balcony giving out over a small garden, and commanding more distantly the harbor and town lights below. From somewhere in the garden came the splashing of a small fountain.

Here Von Ritz left his charge to himself, silently departing with a bow. For a while the Spaniard remained alone. The room was not so brightly illuminated as many through which he had come on his way across the Palace. Light filtered through swinging lamps of wrought metal encrusted with prisms of green and amber and garnet. The Moorish scheme depends in part upon its shadows. Finally a gentleman entered from a balcony. He was neither in uniform nor in evening dress. His face was smooth-shaven and pleasing.

Blanco fancied this was a secretary or attendant of some sort, and was conscious of slight surprise that as he entered the place he smoked a cigarette with a freedom scarcely fitting the King's personal chambers. At the window the gentleman halted and looked Blanco over with a frank but not offensive curiosity. Manuel returned the gaze, wondering where he had seen the face before, yet unable to identify it. Then the newcomer crossed and proffered the Spaniard a cigarette from a gold case, which the *toreador* declined with a shake of his head.

"*Gracias, Señor,*" he said, "but I am waiting for the King."

The other smiled, and the visitor noticed that even in smiling his lips fell into lines of sadness.

"None the less," he said pleasantly, "a man may as well have the solace of tobacco while he waits—even though he awaits a King."

The Andalusian once more shook his head, and the other continued to study him with that undisguised interest which his eyes had worn from the first.

"So you are one of the two men," he said, "who learned what all the secret agents of the Throne failed to unearth. Incidentally it is to you that the present King owes not only his Crown, but his life as well." He paused.

"After all," he went on, "it is neither your fault nor Mr. Benton's that the King could have done very well without either the Crown or his life. You restored something which perhaps he held worthless.... But that is his own misfortune."

Blanco's expressive face mirrored a shade of resentment. He had come on summons from the King and found himself listening to the familiar, even disrespectful, chatter of some underling who laughed at his Monarch and lightly appraised the value of his life while he smoked cigarettes in the Royal apartments. The Spaniard bowed stiffly.

"I observe you are in the confidence of the King," he said, in a tone not untouched with disapproval.

The other man's lips curled in amusement. After a moment he replied with simple gravity.

"I am the King."

Blanco stood gazing in astonishment. "You—the King!" Then, recognizing that the shaving of a mustache and the change into civilian clothes had made the difference in a face and figure he had seen only on the streets and through shifting crowds, he bowed with belated deference.

Karyl once more held out his case. "Now perhaps you will have a cigarette?"

The *toreador* took one and lighted it slowly. The King went on.

"My sole pleasure is pretending that I am not a Monarch. Between ourselves, I should prefer other employment. You, for example, I am told have won fame in the bull ring—and it was fame you earned for yourself."

Blanco flushed, then, bethinking himself of the fact that he had been brought here presumably with a purpose, he ventured to suggest: "Your Majesty wished to see me about some matter?"

The other shook his head.

"No," he said slowly, "it was not really I who sent for you. It was Her Majesty, the Queen."

Before he had time for response the *toreador* caught the sound of a shaken curtain behind him, but since he stood facing the King he did not turn.

Karyl, however, looked up, and then swiftly crossed the room. As he passed, Blanco wheeled to face him and was in time to see him holding back the portières of a door for the Queen to enter.

She was gowned in black with the sparkle of passementerie and jet, and at her breast she wore a single red rose. As she stood for a moment on the threshold, despite the majesty of her slender poise it appeared to Blanco that her grace was rather that of something wild and free and that the Palace seemed to cage her. But that may have been because, as she paused, her hands went to her breast and a furrow came between her brows, while the corners of her lips drooped wistfully like a child's.

The King stooped to kiss her hand, and she turned toward him with a smile which was pallid and which did not dissipate the unhappiness of her face. Then Karyl straightened and said to Blanco, who felt himself suddenly grow awkward as a muleteer: "The Queen."

Manuel dropped on one knee. At a gesture from Cara he rose and waited for her to speak. Karyl himself halted at the door for a moment, then came slowly back into the room. He picked up from a tabouret a decoration of the Star of Galavia, and, crossing over, pinned it to the Spaniard's lapel.

"There!" he said, with a good-humored laugh. "You made me a somewhat valueless present a few days back. You will find that equally useless, Sir Manuel. You may tell Mr. Benton that I envy him such an ally."

With a bow to the Queen, the King left the apartment.

For a moment the girl stood at the door, with the same expression and the same silence, unbroken by her since her entrance, then she turned to the Spaniard and spoke directly. Her voice held a tremor.

"How is he?"

"I have not seen him since the day on the mountain," returned Manuel.

"He has, in you, a very true friend."

"Your Majesty, I am his servant," deprecated the toreador.

"If I had friends like you," she smiled, "it would matter little what they called themselves. And yet, if there is but one like you, I had rather that that one be with him. I want you to go to him now and remain with him."

"Your Majesty, *Señor* Benton left me here to watch for recurring dangers. I am now satisfied that nothing threatens, at least for the present. I might, as Your Majesty suggests, better be with him."

"Yes—yes—with him!" she eagerly agreed; then her voice took on the timbre of anxiety. "I am afraid. Sometimes I am afraid for him. He is not a coward, but there are times when we all become weak. I appoint you, Sir Manuel—" the girl smiled wanly—"I appoint you my Ambassador to be with him and watch after him—and, Sir Manuel—" her voice shook a little with very deep feeling—"I am giving you the office I had rather have than all the thrones in Christendom! Will you accept it?"

She held out her hand, and taking it reverently in his own, the Andalusian bowed low over it. He did not kneel, for now he was the Ambassador in the presence of his Sovereign. "With all the Saints for my witnesses," he declared fervently, "I swear it to Your Majesty."

There was gratitude in her eyes as they met the whole-heartedness of the pledge in his. For a moment she seemed unable to speak, though there was no dimness of tear-mist in her pupils. She stood very upright and silent, and her breathing was deep. Then slowly her hands came up and loosened the flower at her breast.

"The King has decorated you, Sir Manuel," she said. "I don't think Mr. Benton would care for knighthood—and I could not confer it—but sometime—not now—some day after you have both departed from Galavia, give him this. Tell him it may have a message which I may not put in words. If he can read the heart of a rose deeply enough, perhaps he can find it there."

When Blanco had carefully folded the emblem of his embassy in paper and deposited it in his breast pocket, she gave him her hand again, and, turning, went out through the same door that she had entered.

Back in the town, Blanco had certain investigations to make. He knew Von Ritz's men had been too late to capture the Duke, and that the Countess Astaride had sailed by the steamer leaving for French and Italian ports. Wherever these two conspirators should meet would become the next point to watch.

Blanco felt sure that Louis would be willing to drop back into the routine of his life in Paris, freshly stocked with pessimistic memories of how a crown had slipped through his fingers. It would take driving to prevent him lagging into the inertia of sentimental brooding. On the other hand, he knew that the Countess Astaride, having gone so far, would never again relinquish her ambitions. He knew the temper of the Countess's mind from various bits of gossip he had heard and now also from what he had seen. He knew that, while she was entirely willing to participate in a murder plot to further her designs, she was not fired solely by a lust for power. More deeply she was actuated by her wish to make Louis Delgado a man of potentiality because she loved Louis Delgado.

That love might evidence itself in savagery toward men who obstructed the road which her lover must travel to a crown, but it was a ferocity born of love for the Pretender.

Since this was true it was not probable that she would allow the matter to end where it stood. Even if she were willing, it was more than certain that Jusseret had not entered into the undertaking without some sufficient end in view. Having entered it, he would not relinquish it because the first attempt had been bungled.

That same night Manuel sent a message to the *Isis*, saying that he was sailing the following morning by the Genoa steamer and asking that the yacht meet the ship and take him on board. Having done that much, he went to the hotel where the Countess had stopped and told the clerk that he had news of importance to communicate to Madame the Countess, and that he wished to learn her present address. The clerk, like all Puntal, was ignorant of what important matters had just missed happening, but he had instructions from this lady to assume ignorance as to her destination. Blanco, however, showed the seal ring which she had said would prove a passport to her presence and which Benton had left with him. He was promptly informed that she had taken passage for Villefranche, and had ordered her mail forwarded there in care of the steamship agency.

CHAPTER XVI

THE AMBASSADOR BECOMES ADMIRAL

More suggestive of a stowaway than a millionaire, thought Blanco the following afternoon, when he had come over the side of the *Isis* and sought out the owner of the yacht. Benton had turned hermit and withdrawn to the most isolated space the vessel provided. It was really not a deck at all—only a space between engine-room grating and tarpaulined lifeboats on what was properly the cabin roof. Here, removed from the burnished and ship-shape perfection of the yacht's appointment, he lay carelessly shaven and more carelessly dressed.

The lazily undulating Mediterranean stretched unbroken save for the yacht's stack, funnels and stanchions, in a sight-wide radius of blue. Overhead the sky was serene. Here and there, in fitful humors, the sea flowed in rifts of a different hue.

The sun was mellow and the breeze which purred softly in the cables overhead came with the caressing breath that blows off the orange groves of Southern Spain. Ahead lay all the invitation of the south of France; of the Riviera's white cities and vivid countryside; of Monte Carlo's casinos and Italy's villas. Beyond further horizons, waited the charm of Greece, but the man lay on an old army blanket, clad in bagging flannels and a blue army shirt open at the throat. His arms were crossed above his eyes, and he was motionless, except that the fingers which gripped his elbows sometimes clenched themselves and the bare throat above the open collar occasionally worked spasmodically.

Blanco had come quietly, and his canvas shoes had made no sound. For a time he did not announce himself. He was not sure that Benton was awake, so he dropped noiselessly to the deck and sat with his hands clasped about his knees, his eyes moodily measuring the rise and fall of the glaringly white stanchions above and below the sky-line. At frequent intervals they swept back to the other man, who still lay motionless. It was late afternoon and the smoke-stack shadows pointed off in attenuated lines to the bow while the sky, off behind the wake, brightened into the colors of sunset. Finally Benton rose. The unexpected sight of Blanco brought a start and an immediate masking of his face, but in the first momentary glimpse the Andalusian caught a haggard distress which frightened him.

"I didn't know you had come," said Benton quietly. "How long have you been here?"

"I should say a half-hour, *Señor*," replied Manuel, casually rolling a cigarette.

"Why didn't you rouse me? I'm not very amusing, but even I could have relieved the dullness of sitting there like a marooned man on a derelict."

"Dullness?" inquired the *toreador* with a lazy lift of the brows. "It is ease, *Señor*, and ease is desirable—at sea."

The American sat cross-legged on the deck and held out his hand for a cigarette. When he asked a question he spoke in matter-of-fact tones. He even laughed, and the Andalusian chatted on in kind, but secretly and narrowly he was watching the other, and when he had finished his scrutiny he told himself that Benton had been indulging in the dangerous pastime of brooding.

"Tell me—everything," urged the yacht-owner. "What are the revolutionists doing and how is—how are things?" Carefully he avoided directing any question to the point on which his eagerness for news was poignant hunger.

When Blanco told how Louis had left Galavia just before the soldiers reached the lodge, Benton's face darkened. "That was fatal blundering," he complained. "So long as Delgado is at large the Palace is menaced. If they had taken him, and held him under surveillance, the *Cabinet Noir* would be disarmed. Now they will try again."

Blanco nodded.

"There is no charge they can make against him," he mused. "They cannot bring him back because the government cannot admit its peril. Outwardly his bill of health is clean. Assuredly when they let him slip, *Señor*, they committed a grave error."

Benton rose and paced the deck in deep reflection. At last he halted and spread his hands in a gesture half-despairing.

"My God!" he said in a low voice. "The anxiety will drive me mad! You saw their methods. An entire cortége was to be blown into the air—just to kill Karyl. Next time, what will they attempt?" He broke off with a shudder.

"I have seen the Queen," said Blanco slowly.

Benton wheeled. For an instant his face lighted, then he leaned forward. He said nothing, but his whole attitude was a question.

"You behold in me, Sir Manuel Blanco," began the Andalusian grandly. Then, slipping his arm through that of the other man, he began leading him around the deck. When he had finished his narrative, he said: "I begin my office as Ambassador by delivering this packet." From his pocket he produced the paper-wrapped rose. "I was instructed to give it to you at some future time. Possibly, *Señor*, I am over-prompt. Lawyers and diplomats should be deliberate."

The Mediterranean day had died slowly from east to west while the men had talked, and the last shred of glowing sky was darkening into the sea at the edge of the world astern, when Benton greedily thrust out his hand for the packet.

"*Gracias*," he said bluntly, and turning away went precipitously to his cabin.

After dinner, when the Captain had betaken himself to the bridge and the smoke from the Spaniard's cigarettes and Benton's pipe had begun to wreathe clouds against the ceiling-beams, Blanco broached his diplomacy.

In the dulled expressionlessness of the face opposite him and the stoop of the shoulders, Manuel read a need for an active antidote against the corrosive poison of despair.

"Where are we going now, *Señor*?"

Benton shrugged his shoulders.

"'*Quien sabe!*' as you say in Spain. We are simply cruising, drifting, keeping out of sight of land."

"And drifting is the precise thing, *Señor*, which we must not do. I have hitherto done without question what you have said. Now I hold a new dignity." There was a momentary flash of teeth as he smiled. "As Ambassador, I make a request. May I be permitted to take entire control of affairs for a brief time? Also, will you for a few days obey *my* instructions, without question?"

Benton looked across the table at the dark face half-obscured behind a blue fog of cigarette smoke. After a moment he smiled.

"Admiral," he said, "issue your orders."

"You will instruct the Captain," said Manuel promptly, "to head at once for Villefranche. There you, *Señor*, will leave the yacht, and I will go with it to Monte Carlo. I wish to be as soon as possible in the casino where the drone of the *croupier* and the clink of outflowing *louis d'or* constitute the national refrain."

Benton's eyes narrowed in perplexity. On his face was written curiosity, but he had agreed to ask no questions. He unhesitatingly put his finger on the electric bell.

"Ask the Captain to come here as soon as he is at leisure," he directed when the steward had responded to the call.

"Good," commended Blanco. Then with a sorrowful shake of his head he commiserated: "I am sorry that you are to be denied the excitement of the *rouge et noir* and the *trente et quarente* of the gold table, *Señor*, but if the Countess Astaride and Louis should meet there, the lady would know you. I fancy that she will not again mistake you for someone else. As for myself, neither of them yet knows me."

"Are they at Monte Carlo?" Benton sat suddenly upright, and Blanco had the first reward of his diplomacy, as he noted the quickening interest in the questioning eyes.

"I am only guessing, *Señor.* If the guess is good, I may learn something. What is in my mind, may fail. If you are willing to trust me I would rather not reveal it now."

"And I?" questioned Benton. "Have I any part to play in this, or do you go it alone?"

Blanco leaned forward.

"It may be necessary to have someone near enough to the Palace in Puntal to insure immediate action—action to be taken on the instant.... You must return to the city, *Señor*.... It will be for only a few days. The Grand Palace Hotel is above the town in large gardens.... If you choose you can remain there with your presence absolutely unknown, so far as the city proper is concerned. Also, the Marconi office has a station in the hotel grounds. With a code which we have yet to arrange, I can keep in touch with you...."

The next day Benton was a passenger by steamer from Villefranche to Puntal.

The Grand Palace Hotel, dominating its own acres of subtropical gardens, looks down on the city as one seated on an eminence commands the common things at his feet. Between its grounds and the scalloped bay, run the huddled habitations of the town's water-front, with its delicately tinted walls and riotously colored gardens invading every crevice.

Following the semicircle of the bay, the eye commands that other eminence where the King's Palace shuts itself in austerely at the very center of the arc. Through the clustered, tea-sipping loungers on the galleries and terraces Benton made his way several days later, wearing the studiously affected unconcern of the tourist; an unconcern which he found it desperately difficult to assume in Puntal.

Driven by a growing and intense desire to put distance between himself and all alien humanity, he turned into a narrow, steeply climbing street which ran twisting between toy-houses and vine-cumbered garden-walls, until at last it lost its right to be called a street and became merely a narrow, trail-like path up the mountain-side. The wanderer climbed interminably. He took no thought of destination and satisfied himself with the physical exertion of the laborious going.

His heart pounded faster as he attained the altitude of the pine woods where he seemed to have left humanity behind him. Once or twice he saw a shy, half-wild child who fled from its task of gathering fagots at his approach, to gaze at him out of startled eyes from a safe distance.

Occasionally he would stop to look down, from some coign of vantage, at cascading threads of water tumbling into the gorge below, or at a châlet-like house perched far beneath in its trim patch of agriculture. Finally he stretched himself indolently on a carpet of pine needles at the brink of a drop to the valley. Then, with a sense of recognition, he saw the tumbled-down gate of the King's driveway below him to the left, and his face became set and miserable as memory began its work of tearing open wounds not yet old.

Suddenly there drifted up a chorus of children's laughter. He sat up suddenly and looked about, but no one was in sight. Again he heard an unmistakable peal of shrill, childish merriment, seemingly close at hand. He lay flat and looked over the ledge, holding on to a root of a gnarled pine that grew far out at the marge.

Under him, not more than twenty yards below, on a similar natural platform, sat a circle of peasant children, their eyes large with wonderment and interest. In their center, also seated on the earth, was the Queen of Galavia. She was dressed in a short walking skirt and a blue jersey, and as the man gripped the pine root to which he held, and gazed over, she lifted an outstretched finger of a gauntleted hand in illustration of some particularly wonderful point of what was palpably a particularly wonderful fairy story. A third burst of delight came from the listening and responsive auditors, who had no idea by whom they were being entertained.

The peasants of Galavia speak Portuguese. As Benton shifted his position so that he could eavesdrop without being discovered, he found that he could catch some of the words.

"Tell us another story—" piped a high treble voice, "—a story about the beautiful Princess who married the King." The demand was seconded by an immediate clamor of eager voices.

The girl rose unsteadily and shook her head. For a moment she stood looking off over the miles of sea with her hands at her breast and her eyes clouded, oblivious of the small companions of her truancy. She stretched out both strong young arms toward the Mediterranean.

Then she heeded the children's clamor again and, turning to them, she laughed.

"No, no!" she teasingly answered, and the man above realized for the first time that Portuguese is a tongue of liquid music. "These are fairy stories without Princesses. These are perfectly good fairy stories, you know." Then with a sudden burst of confidence, "In really-truly life, Princesses are not much good. Don't any of you ever be a Princess if you can help it!" After planting this seed of treasonable ideas she turned away, adding: "No, no, no! I've run away and I must go back. To-morrow we will have a wonderful story—but no more to-day."

Slowly she made her way down to the old gate, stopping twice to look out to the sea, and above her, choking off the shout that clamored at his lips, the man sat motionless and gave no intimation of his presence.

Finally he rose and made his way unsteadily back to the city. He walked slowly down between the wine-shops, noisy with laughter, to the road along the bay. Immersed in reflection and forgetful of his resolution to keep as much as possible out of sight, he went openly and conspicuously along the street that overhangs the water, where at sunset all Puntal promenades. It was only when a detachment of soldiers in the familiar opera-bouffe uniform went clanking by to change the guard at the Palace gates that he remembered he was to have remained inconspicuous. With a sense of chagrin for his indiscretion, he turned into a side street which sloped upward toward his hotel. This street was so little used that between its cobble stones tender sprigs of grass made the way as green as a turf course.

CHAPTER XVII

BENTON CALLS ON THE KING

There were several things to harrow Benton's thoughts aside from the ingenious tortures of memory. Blanco should have arrived at Monte Carlo on the day of their separation. Benton himself had proceeded slowly to Puntal and had now been an isolated guest at the Grand Palace Hotel for two days, yet he had heard nothing from Manuel. Still the man from Cadiz had not been idly cruising. The *Isis* had duly dropped her anchor in the ultramarine waters where the rock of Monaco juts out like a beckoning finger, and Monte Carlo spreads the marble display of its rococo façades at the feet of the Maritime Alps.

That night, in the most detailed perfection of evening dress, he wandered good-humoredly, yet aloof, through the crowds. He haunted the groups that swarmed about the busy wheels in the casino. He mingled with the diners upon the terraces of the principal hotels. He brushed elbows with the strollers along the promenade and about the *Cercle des Etrangers*, and all the while his studiously alert eyes wandered with seeming vacancy of expression over the faces of the men and women whom he passed.

Safe in the surety of being himself unknown, he trained his countenance into the ennui of one who has no object beyond killing the hour and contributing his quota to the income of the syndicate.

The evening was wasted, together with a few *louis*, and the next morning found the Spaniard scrutinizing every face along the *Promenade des Anglais* at Nice. Then he searched Cannes and Mentone, but by evening he was back again in the sacred City of Black and Red.

As he disembarked from the yacht's launch and came up the white stairs to the landing-stage, his eyes were still indolently wandering, but before he reached the level of the *Boulevard de la Condamine*, the expression changed with the suddenness of discovery into a glint almost triumphant. It was only with strong effort that he banished the satisfied light from his pupils and forced them to wander absently again, along the glitter and color of the palm-lined promenade.

For Manuel had seen a slender, well-groomed figure leaning on the coping of the sea-wall and gazing out with obvious amusement on the life of the harbor. Although the Spaniard did not allow himself a second glance, he knew that his search was ended. The attention of the man above was dreamily fixed on the bay where a dozen darting motor-boats cut swift courses hither and thither. His attitude was graceful. His bearing might have been almost noble except for a deplorable lack of frankness which spoiled otherwise fine eyes, and a self-indulgent weakness which marred the angle of the chin.

The Bay at Monte Carlo is a haven for luxurious craft. Now the Prince of Monaco's yacht lay at anchor and several others, hardly less handsome, rode snugly offshore, but with the enthusiasm of a connoisseur the tall gentleman disregarded all the rest and let his admiring gaze dwell on the *Isis*.

The face was studiously altered. Where there had been a full mustache there was now only a thinly clipped line, waxed and uptilting in needle points. It had been dark brown. Now it was black. The hair formerly brushed straight back from the forehead now showed beneath the hat-band. The Van Dyke which had masked the receding tendency of the chin was shaven away. Evidently the gentleman wished to present a changed appearance to the world, but the visionary eyes were unmistakably those of Louis, the Dreamer, and in lapses of thought the fingers of the right hand nervously twisted and untwisted, after the manner of an old personal trick.

As Blanco came up the stairs he brushed clumsily against the stranger and paused to apologize.

"I am inexcusably awkward," he avowed with engaging contriteness.

The Duke protested that it was not worth mention, and added with a smile, "I noticed that you came from that yacht. I think she is one of the most beautiful little vessels I have ever seen."

"Thank you, Monsieur." Blanco was apparently much flattered. "She is American built, and has some appointments which I have not seen elsewhere." Then smilingly, but in hot haste, he rushed away.

During the course of the evening the Andalusian contrived to throw himself repeatedly across the Duke's path. On each occasion he appeared to be in great haste and under the necessity of immediate departure, though he never left without a cordial word of recognition. He played his game so adroitly that at the end of the evening the Duke felt as though he and the stranger from the American-built yacht were old and pleasant acquaintances.

It was as they stood watching the stiffer gambling of the elect in the upper room of the Casino, after the wheels below had ceased to spin, that the tall gentleman turned to Blanco.

"How do you say? Would a cup of coffee or a glass of wine go amiss?"

Without a trace of eagerness, the Andalusian assented and a few minutes later he found himself across a café table at the Nouvel Hôtel de Paris; listening to Louis, the Dreamer's soft voice, and watching the slender fingers which nervously toyed with a Sévres cup.

"She is extremely beautiful in her lines," Louis was declaring. "I am fond of yachts that are properly built. I am planning one myself, and each new vessel holds for me a fresh interest."

"Ah, indeed!" The Spaniard was delighted. "Then we have fallen upon a common enthusiasm. I am never so happy as when talking to a keen yachtsman." Yet so long as the conversation threatened those nautical technicalities in which he was utterly deficient, he managed to let the other do the talking.

Manuel at last set down his cup and, looking up with a flash, as of sudden inspiration, suggested: "But doubtless you will be stopping in Monte Carlo a day or two? Possibly you will do me the honor of inspecting the boat?"

The other protested that his friend was too good. He regarded himself highly honored. He would be most charmed. But apparently the idea was developing and Blanco was conceiving even more extended notions of hospitality.

"Stay!" he suddenly exclaimed. "Why not breakfast with me, on board, to-morrow at twelve? The launch will be at the landing at eleven forty-five. I could take you cruising for a few knots, and let you test her sailing qualities, returning in abundant time for dinner and the amusements of the evening."

Louis gave the matter a moment's reflection, then declared that the programme was delightful. He would not be engaged until the evening.

Blanco laughed uproariously. "It is most amusing," he declared. "I have had supper with you—you are to breakfast with me, and I have not yet told you my name!" He was searching for a card-case, which seemingly he had misplaced. "I cannot find a card. No matter, my name is Sir Manuel Blanco."

The Duke smiled as he rose from the table and took up hat and cane. "I was equally forgetful," he said. "My name is Monsieur Breuillard."

The following day had advanced well into the afternoon, and Monsieur Breuillard had punctuated with graceful compliment each point of excellence in the equipment of the *Isis*, when Blanco led the way into the small smoking saloon.

"Sailing qualities may not have been fairly tested," admitted Sir Manuel, "since the sea was serene, the sky brilliant, and the breeze insufficient to ruffle the water."

"The more charming, Monsieur!" exclaimed the guest, whose mood after a pleasing day was mellow and complacent.

Blanco waved Monsieur Breuillard to an easy chair and pointed out cigars. As chance would have it, he stood before the door, which he had just closed.

"By the way—Your Grace—" He broke off abruptly to mark the effect of the title on the other man. Evidently he found it highly pleasing for he smiled as the Dreamer winced and came violently to his feet, pale and rigid, but as yet too astounded for speech.

"I did not tell you, did I," went on the Spaniard, "that I have been Sir Manuel Blanco only a few days, and that the title was conferred on me by your royal kinsman, Karyl of Galavia, for a trifling service in confounding his enemies? Before that I was a *matador* in Andalusia."

Delgado stood petrified, his features livid and his eyes blazing with rage. An instinct warned him that to surrender to passion would be only to trap himself more deeply. The man blocking the door filled its breadth with his strong shoulders. Louis turned his head and his eyes caught through the open porthole a glimpse of the receding shore-line of the Riviera. Blanco followed the glance and smiled.

"We shall be losing shore in a short time," he calmly announced. "May I have the honor of showing Your Grace to your stateroom?"

On the next evening Benton emerged from his rooms at the Grand Palace Hotel in Puntal, and threading his way through the loungers on the galleries, sought out a remote corner of the garden, where, under a blossom-freighted vine, he could hear the surge of the sea, and, in a tempered softness, the Viennese waltz of the hotel band. Under him the harbor mirrored lights along the shore and those of ships at anchor. At a distance the windows of the Palace could be seen.

"I beg your pardon—"

Benton recognized the coldly modulated voice before he glanced up at the cloaked figure.

"Colonel Von Ritz," he said, "I am honored."

Von Ritz bowed.

"His Majesty requests that you will do him the honor of coming to the Palace with me—now."

Despite the form of request in which the summons was couched, Von Ritz clothed it in a coldness that brought to Benton's mind the implacable politeness of an arrest. At the hint he stiffened.

"If His Majesty requests my presence," he replied with some shortness, "it will be a pleasure to present myself at once. If—" he paused and looked at the stiffly erect figure before him, "if the peremptory tone you assume is a part of your instruction, I must remind you that I am an American citizen, entirely free to accept or decline invitations—even when they come from the Palace."

Von Ritz replied with unruffled gravity.

"If it will add to your sense of security, Mr. Benton, I shall be pleased to drive you to your Legation and to have your government's representative accompany us."

Benton flushed. "I was not speaking from any sense of personal insecurity," he explained. "But I wished you to understand the manner in which I prefer to be approached."

The Colonel waited with perfect courtesy for the American to finish, then he went on in the same distantly polite tone and manner. "I had not quite finished delivering my message when you—when you began to speak. His Majesty instructs me to say that if you will accompany me to the Palace he will regard it as a courtesy and will be grateful. He commands me to add that he does not send this message officially or as coming from the Court. It is simply that the Count Pagratide wishes to see you and that it is obviously impossible for His Majesty—for the Count Pagratide—to call on you here."

Benton was irritated with himself for his display of temper, and more irritated with Von Ritz for his calm superiority of manner. His murmured apology was offered with no very good grace as he turned to follow the other's lead. Opposite the hotel entrance he stopped.

"Colonel," he said, "I have been awaiting news from Manuel Blanco. He may send a message or come himself, and if so it may be vital for him to establish instant communication with me."

"Certainly," agreed Von Ritz. "I would suggest that you introduce my aide, who may be trusted, at the hotel and that he be instructed to bring you any message. By that means, *Señor* Blanco, or his news, can follow you directly to the Palace—and it does not become necessary to take others into your confidence."

The same young Captain who had summoned Blanco in the Casino was left to act as messenger and Benton, following the officer through a side gate and into a side street, stepped into a closed carriage.

"I had not supposed that the Palace knew of my presence in Puntal," commented the American as he took his seat opposite the Colonel of Cavalry.

"You were seen on the promenade. It was reported from several sources," Von Ritz made answer. "Also," he added as an afterthought, "we knew of your arrival two hours after you reached Puntal. You registered at the hotel under your own name."

"Does the Queen also know of my presence?" asked Benton.

"No," was the brief reply.

For the remainder of the drive conversation died. The two men sat mutely opposite each other as the carriage jolted over the cobble-stoned streets, until the driver turned into the castle gates.

Then Von Ritz again leaned forward.

"Mr. Benton," he explained, "it happens that this evening a ball is being given at the Palace for the members of the Diplomatic Corps. His Majesty, supposing that you would desire a quiet reception, instructed me to take you to the gardens of his private suite where he will shortly join you; unless," added Von Ritz courteously, "you prefer the Throne-room and dancing *salles*?"

Benton's reply was prompt.

"I believe I am to see the Count Pagratide," he answered. "I am grateful to the Count for arranging that I might be secluded."

Blanco had gone into some detail in describing the chamber where he had met the King, and later the Queen. Benton now recognized the place to which he was conducted, from that description. As before, the room was empty and the portières of the wide windows were partly drawn. Through the opening he could see the small area perching on a space redeemed from the solid rock. Dark masses against the sky marked the palms of the garden, and through the window drifted the splashing of a fountain mingled with the distant strains of the same Viennese waltz that the hotel band had been playing. That year you might have heard it from the Golden Gate to Suez and back again from Suez to the Golden Gate.

CHAPTER XVIII

IN WHICH THE SPHINX BREAKS SILENCE

Left alone, Benton spent ten minutes in the room, then passed through the window to the balcony and went down into the miniature garden. His face was hot and his pulses heightened. The garden was gratefully cool and quiet.

From the window, through which he had come, a broad shaft of tempered luminance fell across the fountain and laid a zone of soft light athwart the low stone benches surrounding it. Then it caught, and faintly edged with its glow, the granite balustrade at the shoulder of the cliff. Elsewhere the little garden was enveloped in the velvet blackness of the night, against which the points of town and harbor lights, far below, were splinters of emerald and ruby. The moon would not rise until late.

The American strolled over to the shaded margin which was unspoiled by the light. He brushed back the hair from his forehead and let the sea breeze play on his face.

Finally a light sound behind him called his attention inward. The King and Von Ritz stood together in the doorway. Both were in dress uniform. Karyl, even at the side of the soldierly Von Ritz, was striking in the white and silver of Galavia's commanding general. Across his breast glinted the decorations of all the orders to which Royalty entitled him.

The King, with a deep breath not unlike a sigh, came forward to the fountain. There he halted with one booted foot on the margin of the basin and his white-gauntleted hands clasped at his back. He had not yet seen Benton, who now stepped out of the shadow to present himself. As he came into view Karyl raised his eyes and nodded with a smile.

"Ah, Benton," he said, "so you came! Thank you."

The American bowed. He wished to observe every proper amenity of Court etiquette. He was still chagrined by the memory of his rudeness to Von Ritz, yet he was determined that if Karyl had sent for him as the Count Pagratide, he must receive him on equal terms and without ceremony.

"Certainly," he replied. Then with a short laugh he added: "I have never before been received by a crowned head. If my etiquette proves faulty, you must score it against my ignorance—not my intention."

"I sent for you," said Karyl slowly, as the eyes of the two men met in full directness, "and you were good enough to come. I am a crowned head—yes—that is my damned ill-fortune. Let us, for God's sake, in so far as we may, forget that! Benton, back there—" his voice suddenly rose and took on a passionate tremor as he lifted one gauntleted hand in a sweep toward the west—"back there in your country, where you were a grandee of finance and I an impecunious foreigner, there was no ceremony between us. If we can forget this livery"—Karyl savagely struck his breast—"if you will try to forget that you are looking at a toy King, fancifully trimmed from head to heel in braid and medals—then perhaps we can talk!"

"Your Majesty—" demurred Von Ritz in a tone of deep protest.

The King swept his arm back as one who brushes an unimportant intruder into the background.

"And we must talk," went on Karyl vehemently, "as two men, not as one man and a puppet."

The American stood looking on at the violence of the King's outburst with a sense of deep sympathy. Again the Colonel stepped forward with an interposed objection.

"If I may suggest—" he began in an emotionless inflection which fell in startling contrast with the surcharged vehemence of the other. Then he halted in the midst of his sentence as Karyl wheeled passionately to face him.

"My God, Colonel!" cried the King. "There is not a debt of gratitude in life that I do not owe to you—I and my house! I am crushed under my obligations to you. You have been our strength, our one loyal support, and yet there are times when you madden me!" The officer stood waiting, respectful, impersonal, until the flood of words should subside, but for a while Karyl swept agitatedly on.

"You wear a sword, Von Ritz, which any monarch in Europe would hire at your own price. Any government would let you name what titles and honors you wished in payment—"

"Your Majesty!"

"Forgive me, I know your sword is not for sale. I mean no such intimation. I mean only that it has a value. I mean you are a man, and the game to you is the large one of statecraft. It is really you who rule this Kingdom. Ah, yes, you remonstrate, but I tell you it is true, and the damnable shame is that it is not a Kingdom worthy of your genius! You, Von Ritz, are the engine, the motive force—but I—in God's holy name, what am I?"

He raised his hands questioningly, appealingly.

"You," replied the older soldier calmly, "are the King."

"Yes," Karyl caught up the words almost before they had fallen from the lips of the other. "Yes, I am the King. I am the miserable, gilded figurehead out on the prow, which serves no end and no purpose. I am the ornamental symbol of a system which the world is discarding! I am a medieval lay figure upon which to hang these tinsel decorations, these ribbons!"

"Your Majesty is excited."

"No, by God, I am only heartbroken—and I am through!" The King's hands dropped at his sides. The passion died out of his voice and eyes, leaving them those of a man who is very tired. For a moment there was silence. It was broken by the American.

"Pagratide," he asked, "why did you send for me?"

The King stood rigid with the illuminating shaft from the door touching into high-lights the polish of his boots and the burnish of his accouterments. Finally he turned and in a voice now deadly quiet countered with another question.

"Benton, why did you save me?"

The American answered with quiet candor.

"I went into it," he said, "because I feared the danger might threaten Cara. Once in, only a murderer could have turned back."

"So I thought." Karyl nodded his head, then he turned and paced restively up and down the path between the fountain and the balcony. At last he halted fronting the American.

"I wish to God, Benton, you had let that traitor Lapas and his constituents touch their damned button. I wish to God you had let them lift me, amid the stones of *do Freres*, into eternity! But that wish is uncharitable to Von Ritz and the others who must have gone with me." The King broke off with a short laugh. "After all," he added, "of course, as you say, you couldn't do it."

Benton shook his head. "No," he said, "I couldn't do it."

Again Karyl paced back and forth, and again he stopped, facing the American.

"Benton, it is hard for two men to talk in this fashion. Perhaps no two other men ever did. I find myself a jailer to the woman I love—Oh, yes, I am also imprisoned by Royalty but that does not alter matters." The voice shook. The gauntleted hands were tightly gripped, but the speaker went steadily on. "And you love her!"

For an instant Benton looked at the other, hesitant. Then realizing the unquestionable sincerity with which the King spoke, he answered with equal frankness.

"Pagratide—over there—I thought I could enter Paradise. I did look into Paradise. Then I had to set my face back again to the desert—and in the desert one has only memory and hunger and thirst."

"Yours is hunger and thirst—yes!" exclaimed the King of Galavia. "But mine is the hunger and thirst of Tantalus."

There was a low pained exclamation from the balcony and both men wheeled in recognition of the voice and the shadow that divided the band of light in the doorway.

The Queen stood on the low sill and though her head and figure were only sketched in shade against the tempered luminance at her back her exclamation told them that she had heard. She stood in the unbroken sweep of her Court gown. Her slim hands gripped the ermine which fell from her shoulders to the floor and slowly crushed it between clenched fingers. About her head the light touched her hair into a soft nimbus.

Karyl stepped impetuously forward and held out his hand to lead her into the garden. Benton, who had involuntarily started toward the balcony at the first sight of her, caught his lip in his teeth and halted where he stood.

The girl remained for a moment, astonished at the sight of the two men, incredulous of what she had heard.

She had slipped away for a moment of respite from the fatiguing requirements of the ball-room. She had come here because she had felt sure that here she could be alone. She had come, driven by the prompting of her heart, to look out to the Mediterranean and wonder where, between its gates at Gibraltar and Suez, Benton might at that moment be. And from the balcony she had seen him in the garden and had heard a part of this talk before the spell of her astounded muteness broke into exclamation.

"You heard what we were saying." Karyl spoke gently, deferentially. "And it seemed to you incredible that we should be confidential on such a subject. It would be so, except that we are both seeking the same end—your service—" he paused, then added miserably—"and your happiness."

She listened in wonderment as she held out her hand to Benton and watched trance-like his lowered head as he bent his lips to her fingers.

"Cara!" Karyl had stepped back and was leaning over, his elbows resting on the stone back of one of the low benches. His fingers tightly grasped the carved ornaments at its top. His words were carefully chosen and measuredly spoken. He knew that if he permitted one expression to escape him unguardedly, with it would slip away the command by which he was curbing mutinous emotions.

"Cara, I happened to be born a Prince, who should one day develop into a King. It chanced that Nature had a sense of humor—so Nature paid me a droll compliment. She gave me a futile ambition to be a man—me, whom she had decided was to be only a King!"

The group stood silent and attentive in a strained tableau, except for Von Ritz, who paced back and forth just beyond the fountain, as though respectfully repudiating the whole unseemly episode.

"Then I fell in love with you," went on the King of Galavia. "You married me—because State reasons demanded it. I could not win your love—he did!" He turned toward Benton, and his voice, though it held its slow control, was bitter.

"Benton, do you fancy this puny game amuses me? Do I not know that you could buy a principality like this for a souvenir of Europe if it happened to please you? The one time I have been allowed to feel a man was in your country, where we met as equal rivals.... No, not equal even then, because you were the winner, I the loser."

"Karyl," the Queen spoke in a low voice, "I can give you loyalty, admiration, respect and my life to use as you see fit to use it. I give as freely as I can. My love I do not refuse—it is just ... just that it is not mine to give." She spoke with unutterable weariness. "I seem to bring only sorrow to those who love me."

"You can give me all but love," Karyl repeated very softly, leaning forward toward her, "and love is all there is! Without it I take all else you give me as a thief takes, without right. If being a King means being your jailer, then I am done with being a King!"

"Your Majesty," cut in Von Ritz sharply, "it is time to terminate this talk. It has no end. It is aimless argument which comes only back to the starting point."

The King wheeled and met the eyes of his adviser. The studied self-control he had maintained since Cara's arrival slipped from him and his voice broke out explosively.

"It has an end!" he cried. "I will show you the end. If I cannot build empire I can do something else, I can throw this damnable little Kingdom down into the chaos it deserves!... I can abdicate to my cousin, Louis Delgado, who wants the throne I don't want!... I can stamp on this tinseled trumpery.... I can break jail!" He turned with an impassioned out-sweeping of his hands. Coming swiftly from behind the bench, he halted tensely before Benton and leaned defiantly forward. "Then I can free her—and by God I shall fight you for her on equal terms, inch by inch, not holding her in duress, but fighting for her free consent. She has been trapped by Fate into marrying me and at heart she rebels. I shall set her free and then by God I will win her back!"

Von Ritz had stood by as the King rushed on in climax after climax of heated words. Now he took one swift stride forward. From his quiet face had fallen every trace of impassiveness. When he spoke his voice trembled with the irresistible eloquence of power and fire.

"My God, boy!" He seized Karyl by his shoulders and wheeled him so that they stood face to face. There was in his manner nothing of deference, nothing of the subordinate. Now he stood transformed, the man of action; the dominant, compelling force before whom littler men must wither. This was no longer Von Ritz the emotionless. It was Von Ritz the King-maker, burning with vitalizing passion.

"My God, boy, are you mad? Do you think other men have never loved and sacrificed themselves for duty—kept unuttered, locked in their hearts, things they were hungry to say?... Do you think that your hard task of Kingship is yours to play with—to desert?... Why, boy, I've taught you your manual of arms, I've drilled you, trained you, watched you grow from childhood. My heart has beaten with joy because you were free of every degenerate trace that has marked and scarred Europe's cancerous Royalty! I've seen you come clean-hearted, straight-minded into man-hood; prepared you to show the world what a Kingdom can be with a clean King—a strong King! I've fitted you to bear a burden which only a man could bear—to remind the world that 'King' means the Man Who Can—and I thought you could do it!" He paused only to draw a long breath, then hastened on again. "Yes, your task is thankless. Your Principality is small, but it is a keystone in Europe's arch. It is such Princelings as you who must send clean blood down to the thrones of to-morrow.... Is that not enough?... Have I built a King, day by day, year by year, idea by idea, only to see him wither and crumple under the first blast? Go on with your task, in God's name! Probably they will murder you ... assassination may at the end be your reward, but only the coward fears the outcome! For God's sake, Karyl, don't desert me under fire!"

He paused with a gesture eloquent of appeal. When next he spoke his voice was slow, deliberate.

"And the other picture! The café tables of Paris are crowded with Royalty that has been; with the miserable children of conquered and abdicated Kings!"

The King dropped exhaustedly to the bench, his fore-arms on his knees, his gloved fingers hanging limp. After a moment he rose again and went to Cara.

"I want to fight for you," he said simply. "I want to free you first—then fight for you."

"Karyl," she answered gently, "if you do *this*, you will enslave my soul, and my imprisonment will be only harder. You will make me a wrecker of governments—a traitor to my duty."

The King turned and looked out to sea.

"I must think," he said in a tired voice. "Perhaps it is only a matter of time. Delgado is free. Perhaps I shall not have to present him with my throne. Conceivably he may come and take it."

Von Ritz approached again and took Karyl's hand. To him a King was, at last analysis, only the best product of the King-maker's craft. He was a King-maker—before him stood a tired boy whom he loved.

"You will fight," he said, "and you will fight with hell's fury. The first step will be to recapture this Pretender. With him in hand—"

"Which is in itself impossible," retorted Karyl.

At the window appeared the young Captain who had been left at the hotel. His hand was at his forehead in salute. Von Ritz went to meet him and in a moment returned for Benton. Together the two men went out. Five minutes later they had come again into the garden. With them came Manuel Blanco.

The bull fighter paused to bow low to the Queen, then to the King. At last he spoke with some diffidence.

"I have taken the very great liberty," he said, "of making the Duke Louis Delgado an enforced guest on the yacht—where he awaits Your Majesty's pleasure."

CHAPTER XIX

THE JACKAL TAKES THE TRAIL

"When the Duke avowed himself to be kidnaped, he committed an error so grave that it can hardly be—overestimated." The speaker used the last word as an afterthought. His first inclination was to say, forgiven.

Monsieur Jusseret sat upright in the brougham, scorning the supporting cushions at his back. His small, shrewd eyes frowned his deep disapproval over the roofs of Algiers outspread below him. He scowled on the gaudy and tatterdemalion color of the native city. He scowled on the smart brilliancy of the French quarter basking along the *Place du Government* and the *Boulevard de la Republique.*

The Countess Astaride leaned back and smiled from the depths of the cushions.

"It is usually a mistake to be made a prisoner," she smiled.

"But such a foolish mistake," quarreled Jusseret. "To permit oneself to be lured into so palpable a trap. It is most absurd."

"Now that it is done," inquired the woman, "is it not almost as absurd to waste time deploring the spilled milk? We must find a way to set him free."

"I have done all that could be done. I have stationed men whom I can trust throughout Puntal and Galavia. They are men Karyl likewise thinks he can trust. The distinction is that I know—where he merely thinks."

"And these men—what have they done?" The Countess laid one gloved hand eagerly on the Frenchman's coat-sleeve.

"These men have gradually and quietly reorganized the army, the bureaucracy, the very palace Guard. We have undermined the government's power, until when the word is passed to strike the blow, a honey-combed system will crumble under its own weight. When Karyl calls on his troops, not one man will respond. Well—" Jusseret smiled dryly—"perhaps I overstate the case. Possibly one man will. I think we will hardly convert Von Ritz."

"Ah, that is good news, Monsieur." The Countess breathed the words with a tremor of enthusiasm.

"It is, however, all useless, Madame—since His Grace is unavailable. In captivity he is absolutely valueless."

"In captivity he has a stronger claim upon our loyalty than in power!"

The dark-room diplomat regarded her with a disappointed smile.

"For a clever woman, *Comptesse*, who has heretofore played the game so brilliantly, you have grown singularly unobservant. I am not a crusader, liberating captive Christian knights. I am France's servant, playing a somewhat guileful game which is as ancient as Ulysses, and subject to certain definite rules."

"Yes, but—"

"But, my dear lady, this revolution I have planted—nourished and cultivated to ripeness—I cannot harvest it. Outside Europe must not appear interested in this matter. If the Galavian people led by a member of the Galavian Royal House revolts! *Bien!* More than *bien*—excellent!" Jusseret spread his palms. "But unless there is a leader, there can be no revolution. No, no, Louis should have kept out of custody."

The Countess leaned forward with sudden eagerness.

"And if I free him? If I devise a way?"

The Frenchman turned quickly from contemplation of the landscape to her face.

"Ah!" he exclaimed. "Once more you are yourself; the cleverest woman in Europe, as, always, you are the most charming!"

"Do you know where Monsieur Martin may be found?"

Jusseret looked at her in surprise.

"I supposed he was here, consulting with you. I sent him to you with a letter—recommending him as a useful instrument."

"He was in Algiers, but I sent him away." The Countess laughed. "He wanted money, always money, until I wearied of furnishing his purse."

"Even if he were available he could hardly go to Puntal, Madame," demurred Jusseret. "Von Ritz knows him."

"True." The Countess sat for a time in deep thought.

"There is one man in Puntal," said Jusseret with sudden thought, "who might possibly be of assistance to you. He is not legally a citizen of Galavia. He even has a certain official connection with another government. He is a man I cannot myself approach." Jusseret had been talking in a low tone, too low to endanger being overheard by the *cocher*, but now with excess of caution he leaned forward and whispered a name. The name was José Reebeler.

It was June. Three months had passed since the Grand Duke had steamed into Puntal Harbor as Blanco's prisoner of war. The Duke had since that day been a guest of the King. His goings and comings were, however, guarded with strict solicitude. One day he went after his custom for a stroll in the Palace garden. He was accompanied by two officers of the Palace Guard especially selected by Von Ritz for known fidelity. At the garden gates stood picked sentinels. That evening a fisherman's boat stole out of the harbor. Neither Louis Delgado nor his guard returned. The sentinels failed to respond at roll-call.

As the King and the Colonel listened to the report of the escape, Karyl's face paled a little and the features of Von Ritz hardened. Orders were given for an instant dispatch in cipher, demanding from a secret agent in Algiers all information obtainable as to the movements of the Countess Astaride. The reply brought the statement that the Countess had, several days before, sailed for Alexandria and Cairo.

Von Ritz became preternaturally active, masking every movement under his accustomed seeming of imperturbable calm. At last he brought his report to the King. "It signifies one thing which I had not suspected. Among the men whom I thought I could most implicitly trust, there is treason. How deep that cancer goes is a matter as to which we can only make guesses."

Karyl took a few turns across the floor.

"And by that you mean that we are over a volcano which may break into eruption at any moment?"

Von Ritz nodded.

"And the Queen—" began Karyl.

"I have been thinking of Her Majesty," said the Colonel. "She should leave Puntal, but she will not go, if it occurs to her that she is being sent away to escape danger. Her Majesty's courage might almost be called stubborn."

The King made no immediate response. He was standing at a window, looking out at the serenity of sea and sky. His forehead was drawn in thought. He knew that Von Ritz was right. Had Cara hated him, instead of merely finding herself unable to love him, he knew that the first threat of danger would arouse the ally in her, and that the suggestion of flight would throw her into the attitude of determined resistance. She was like the captain who goes down with his ship, not because he loves the ship, but because his place is on the bridge.

Von Ritz went on quietly.

"God grant that Your Majesty may be in no actual danger. But we must face the situation open-eyed. Your place is here. If by mischance you should fall, there is no reason why—" he hesitated, then added—"why the dynasty should end with you. In Galavia there is no Salic law. Her Majesty could reign. Undoubtedly the Queen should be in some safer place."

The King dropped into a chair and sat for some minutes with his eyes thoughtfully on the floor. Abstractedly he puffed a cigarette. At last he raised his face. It was pale, but stamped with determination.

"There is only one thing to do, Von Ritz. There is one available refuge."

The soldier read the reluctant eyes of the other, and spared him the necessary explanation with a question. "Mr. Benton's yacht?" he inquired.

Karyl nodded. "The yacht."

"I, too, had thought of that, but how can you arrange it, Your Majesty?"

"We must persuade her that she requires a change of scene and that this is the one way she can have it without conspicuousness. It can be given out that she has gone to Maritzburg, and I shall tell her"—Karyl smiled with a cynical humor—"that I am over-weary with this task of Kingship, and that I shall join her within a few days for a brief truancy from the cares of state."

"It may be the safest thing," reflected the officer. "It at least frees our minds of a burdensome anxiety."

"I shall persuade her," declared Karyl. "She can take several ladies-in-waiting and you can accompany her to the yacht and explain to Benton. Direct him to cruise within wireless call and to avoid cities where the Queen might be in danger of recognition. She must remain until we gain some hint as to when and where the crater is apt to break into eruption."

Jusseret was busy. His agencies were at work over the peninsula. It was the sort of conspiracy in which the Frenchman took the keenest delight—purely a military revolution.

The peasant on the mountains, the agriculturist in his buttressed and terraced farm, the grape-grower in his vineyard and the artisan and laborer in Puntal did not know that there was dissatisfaction with the government.

But in the small army and the smaller bureaucracy there was plotting and undermining. Subtle and devious temptations were employed. Captains saw before them the shoulder straps of the major, lieutenants the insignia of the captain, privates the chevrons of the sergeant.

Meanwhile, from a town in southerly Europe, near the Galavian frontier, Monsieur Jusseret in person was alertly watching.

Martin, the "English Jackal," much depleted in fortune, drifting before vagabond winds and hailing last from Malta, learned of the Frenchman's seemingly empty programme. Since his dismissal by the Countess, there had been no employer for his unscrupulous talents. Now he needed funds. Where Jusseret operated there might be work in his particular line. He knew that when this man seemed most idle he was often most busy. Martin had come to a near-by point by chance. He went on to Jusseret's town, and then to his hotel, with the same surety and motive that directs the vulture to its carrion. The Jackal was ushered into the Frenchman's room in the tattered and somewhat disheveled condition to which his recent weeks of vagabondage had subjected him.

Jusseret looked his former ally over with scarcely concealed contempt. Martin sustained the stare and returned it with one coolly audacious.

"I daresay," he began, with something of insolence in his drawl, "it's hardly necessary to explain why I'm here. I'm looking for something to do, and in my condition"—he glanced deprecatingly down at his faded tweeds—"one can't be over nice in selecting one's business associates."

Jusseret was secretly pleased. He divined that before the end came there might be use for Martin, though no immediate need of him suggested itself. There were so few men obtainable who would, without question, undertake and execute intrigue or homicide equally well. It might be expedient to hold this one in reserve.

"We will not quarrel, Monsieur Martin," he said almost with a purr. "It is not even necessary to return the compliment. It is so well understood, why one employs your capable services."

The Englishman flushed. To defend his reputation would be a waste of time.

"*Madame la Comptesse* d'Astaride," explained Jusseret, "has gone to Cairo. She may require your wits as well as her own before the game is played out. Join her there and take your instructions from her." As he spoke the map-reviser began counting bills from his well-supplied purse. Martin looked at them avidly, then objected with a surly frown.

"She sent me away once, and I don't particularly care for the Cairo idea."

"This time she will not send you away." Jusseret glanced up with a bland smile. "And it seems I remember a season, not so many years gone, when you were a rather prominent personage upon the terrace of Shephard's. You were quite an engaging figure of a man, Monsieur Martin, in flannels and Panama hat, quite a smart figure!"

The Englishman scowled. "You delight, Monsieur, in touching the raw spots—However, I daresay matters will go rippingly." He took the bills and counted them into his own purse. "A chap can't afford to be too sentimental or thin-skinned." He was thinking of a couple of clubs in Cairo from which he had been asked to resign. Then he laughed callously as he added aloud: "You see there's a regiment stationed there, just now, which I'd rather not meet. I used to belong to its mess—once upon a time."

Jusseret looked up at the renegade, then with a cynical laugh he rose.

"These little matters *are* inconvenient," he admitted, "but embarrassments beset one everywhere. If one turns aside to avoid his old regiment, who knows but he may meet his tailor insistent upon payment—or the lady who was once his wife?"

He lighted a cigarette, then with the refined cruelty that enjoyed torturing a victim who could not afford to resent his brutality, he added:

"But these army regulations are extremely annoying, I daresay—these rules which proclaim it infamous to recognize one who—who has, under certain circumstances, ceased to be a brother-officer."

The Englishman was leaning across the table, his cheek-bones red and his eyes dangerous.

"By God, Jusseret, don't go too far!" he cautioned.

The Frenchman raised his hands in an apologetic gesture, but his eyes still held a trace of the malevolent smile.

"A thousand pardons, my dear Martin," he begged. "I meant only to be sympathetic."

CHAPTER XX

THE DEATH Of ROMANCE IS DEPLORED

"And yet," declared young Harcourt, "if there still survives, anywhere in the world, a vestige of Romance, this should be her refuge; her last stand against the encroachments of the commonplace."

He spoke animatedly, with the double eagerness of a boy and an artist, sweeping one hand outward in an argumentative gesture. It was a gesture which seemed to submit in evidence all the palpitating colors of Capri sunning herself among her rocks: all the sparkle and glitter of the Bay of Naples spreading away to the nebulous line where Ischia bulked herself in mist against the horizon: all the majesty of the cone where the fires of Vesuvius lay sleeping.

Across the table Sir Manuel Blanco shrugged his broad shoulders.

Benton lighted a cigarette, and a smile, scarcely indicative of frank amusement, flickered in his eyes.

"Do you hold that Romance is on the run?" he queried.

"Where do you find it nowadays?" demanded the boy in flannels. "There!" With the violence of disgust he slammed a Baedeker of Southern Italy down upon the table. "That is the way we see the world in these days! We go back with souvenir postcards instead of experiences, and when we get home we have just been to a lot of tramped-over places. I'll wager that a handful of this copper junk they call money over here, would buy in a bull market all the real adventure any of us will ever know."

The three had been lunching out-doors in a Capri hotel with flagstones for a floor and overhanging vine-trellises for a roof. Chance had thrown this young stranger across their path, and luncheon had cemented an acquaintanceship.

"Who can say?" suggested Benton. "Why hunt Trouble under the alias of Romance? Vesuvius, across there, is as vague and noiseless to-day as a wraith, but to-morrow his demon may run amuck over all this end of Italy! And then—" His laugh finished the speculation.

"And yet," went on the boy, after a moment's pause, "I was just thinking of a chap I met in Algiers a while back and later on the boat to Malta. I ran across him in one of those vile little twisting alleys in the Kasbah quarter where dirty natives sit cross-legged on shabby rugs and eye the 'Infidel dogs' just as spiders watch flies from loathsome webs—ugh, you know the sort of place!" He paused with a slight shudder of reminiscent disgust. "I fancy he has had adventures. We had a glass of wine later down at one of the sidewalk cafés in the *Boulevard de la Republique*. He showed me lots of things that a regular guide would have omitted. The fellow was on his uppers, yet he had been something else, and still knew genteel people. Up on the driveway by the villas, where fashion parades, he excused himself to speak with a magnificently dressed woman in a brougham, and she chatted with him in a manner almost confidential. He told me later she might some day occupy a throne; I think her name was the Countess Astaride."

Benton looked up quickly and his eyes met those of the Spaniard with a swiftly flashed message which excluded Harcourt.

"This fellow and I were on the same boat coming over to Valetta," continued the young tourist. "One night in the smoke-room, the steward was filling the glasses pretty frequently. At last he became confidential."

"Yes?" prompted Benton.

"Well, he told me he had once held a commission in the British Army and had seen service in diplomacy as military attaché. Then he got cashiered. He didn't go into particulars, and of course I didn't cross-question. He recited some weird experiences. He had been a cattle man in Australia and a horse-trader in Syria and had served the Sultan in Turkey. There were lots of things that would have made a good book." The boy's voice took on a note of young ardor. "But the great story was the one he told last. He had stood to win a title of nobility in this two-by-four Kingdom of Galavia, but it had slipped away from him just on the verge of attainment."

Harcourt slowly drained his thin Capri wine and set down the goblet.

"I must watch the time," he remembered at last, drawing out his watch. "I do the Blue Grotto this afternoon.... Well, to continue: This chap gave the name Browne (he insisted that it be Browne with an e), though while he was drunk he called himself Martin.

"He told a long and complicated story of plans in which a King was to lose his life and throne. He said that the secret cabinets of several of the major European governments were interested, and that just as carefully prepared plans were about to be consummated something happened—something mysterious which none of the cleverest agents of the governments had been able to solve. In some unfathomable way someone had discovered everything and stepped between and disarranged. No upheaval followed and of course Browne never won his title. They have never yet learned who saved that throne. Someone is working magic and getting away with it under the eyes of Europe's cleverest detectives."

The boy stopped and looked about to see if his recital had aroused the proper wonderment. Both men gave expression of deep interest. Flattered by the impression he had made, Harcourt went on. "Now you fellows are old travelers—men of the world—I am a kid compared to you. Yet has either of you stumbled on such a story as that? So you see wonderful things do sometimes happen under the surface of affairs with never a ripple at the top of the water. Browne—or Martin—said that the Duke would reign yet—- oh, yes, he said the Powers would see to that!"

"*Señor*, what became of your friend?" inquired Blanco.

"Oh!" the boy hesitated for a moment, then broke into a laugh. "I'm afraid that's an anti-climax. They found that he was simply a nervy stowaway. He had not booked his passage and so—"

"They put him off?"

"Yes, at Malta. Meantime he was stripped to the waist and armed with a shovel in the stoke-hold."

Benton laughed.

"There was another phase to it, though—" began the boy afresh.

At that moment the whistle of the small excursion steamer below broke out in a shrill scream. Young Harcourt hurriedly pushed back his chair and grabbed for his Panama hat. "Cæsar!" he cried, "there's the whistle. I shall miss my boat for the Grotto." And he hastened off with a shout of summons to a crazy victoria that was clattering by empty.

During a long silence Blanco studied the cone of Vesuvius.

"Blanco!" Benton leaned across the table with an anxious frown and stretched out a hand which over-turned the wine glasses. "There was one thing he said that stuck in my memory. He said the Powers would see that in the end Louis had his throne."

The Spaniard shook his head dubiously.

"The Powers have lost their instrument! You forget, *Señor*, that this is underground diplomacy. It must appear to work itself out and the new King must be logical. With Louis a prisoner their meddling hands are bound."

Benton rose and pushed back his chair. His companion joined him and together they passed out through the stone-flagged court and into the road. For fifteen minutes they walked morosely and in silence through the steep streets where the shops are tourist-traps, alluringly baited with corals and trinkets. Finally they came out on the beach where many fishing boats were dragged up on the sand, and nets stretched, drying in the sun.

Then Benton spoke.

"In God's name, Manuel, what do I care who occupies the throne of Galavia? No other man could so block my path as Karyl." Then as one in the confessional he declared shamefacedly: "I have never said it to any man because it is too much like murder, but—sometimes I wish I had reached Cadiz one day later than I did." He drew his handkerchief and wiped the moisture from his forehead.

The Spaniard skillfully kindled a cigarette in the spurt of a match, which the gusty sea-breeze made short-lived.

"And now," he calmly suggested, "it is still possible to let Europe play out her game alone. After all, *Señor*, we are as the young *touristo* indicated—only amateurs."

"And yet, Manuel," the American smiled half-quizzically, "yet we seem foreordained to play bodyguard to Karyl. Fate throws him on our hands."

"We might decline in future to accept the charge."

Benton halted so close to the water's edge that a bit of sea-weed was washed up close to his feet. "Any threat to the throne of Galavia now is also a threat to Her. We must learn what these Powers purpose doing." He threw back his shoulders and his step quickened with the resolution of fresh action.

"Besides," he supplemented, "Delgado is a dreaming degenerate! We must get back into the game."

The Spaniard laughed. "As you say, *Señor*. After all, this mere cruising grows monotonous. Playing the game is better."

When, at twilight that evening, the launch came chugging back to the yacht with the mail from Naples, Benton caught sight of a blue envelope in which he recognized the form of the Italian telegraph. He tore it open and his brows contracted in incredulous wonderment as he read the message.

"Miss Carstow and two other ladies arrive Parker's Hotel Naples Tuesday afternoon. Rely on your meeting her with yacht. She will explain. Be ready to sail immediately on arrival. Address reply Pagratide, care Grand Palace Hotel."

Benton smiled almost happily as he scrawled, in reply, "*Isis* and self at Miss Carstow's service. Waiting under steam. Benton."

CHAPTER XXI

NAPLES ASSUMES NEW BEAUTY

The following day was Tuesday. It found Benton nearer cheerfulness than he had been since the *Isis* had in February pointed her bow eastward for the run across the Atlantic, under sealed orders.

To Blanco the yachtsman announced that he would lunch at Parker's, and evasively asked the Spaniard if he would mind being left alone for the day.

As the coachman, hailed at random from the mob of brigands by the Custom-house entrance, cracked his whip over the bony stallion in the fiacre shafts, Benton began to notice that Naples was altogether charming. He found no refusals for the tatterdemalion vagabonds who pattered alongside to thrust their violets over the carriage door.

At last, as he paced one of the main parlors of the hotel, his eyes riveted on the street entrance, he heard a laugh behind him; a laugh tempered with a vibrant mellowness which was of a sort with no other laugh, and which set him vibrating in turn, as promptly as a tuning-fork answers to its note.

The sound brought him round in such electric haste as almost resulted in collision with the girl behind him.

He was prepared, of course, to find in her incognita no suggestion of Royalty, yet now when he met her standing alone, and could take the hand she held out to him with her heart-breaking, heart-recompensating smile, he felt a distinct sense of astonishment.

"I'm having a holiday," she declared. "It's to be the Queen's day off and you are being allowed to play host with the *Isis*. Do you approve?"

With abandonment to the delight of mere propinquity, he laid away sorrow against the returning time of her absence, as one lays away an umbrella until the next shower.

"Approve?" he mocked. "It's like asking the drowning man if he approves of being picked up."

For a moment her eyes clouded and a droop threatened her lips.

"But," she said in a softer tone, "what if you've got to be thrown back into the sea again?" Then she added, "And, you see, I have. Probably I'm very foolish to come. The prison will only be blacker, but I couldn't stand it. I wanted—" She looked at him with the frankness which has nothing to conceal—"I wanted to forget it all for a little time."

With a frigid salutation, Colonel Von Ritz arrived. As he addressed the American, despite his flawless courtesy, his voice still carried the undercurrent of antagonism which no word of his had ever failed to convey to Benton, since their first meeting in America.

"If Miss Carstow"—he uttered the assumed name with distaste—"will excuse you," he suggested, "I should like a word."

Von Ritz led the way out of doors and between the tables and trellises of the garden until he came upon a spot which seemed to promise the greatest possible degree of privacy. There he stopped and stood looking straight ahead of him.

"All that I now tell you, Mr. Benton"—his voice was even and polite to a nicety, yet distinctly icy—"is of course a message from the King."

"Meaning," Benton smiled with polite indifference, "that your personal communications with me would be few?"

"Meaning," corrected Von Ritz gravely, "that in His Majesty's affairs, I speak only on His Majesty's authority."

"Colonel, I am at your service."

"In the first place," began the Galavian at last, "His Majesty wished me to explain why he has presumed on your further assistance. You are the only man outside Galavia who understands—and whom the King may implicitly trust, trust even with the safety of Her Majesty, the Queen."

"You will convey to the King my appreciation of his confidence." Somehow, between the American and this emissary of Karyl, there could never be any attitude other than that of the utmost formality.

Von Ritz sketched the situation.

"It is important that the world should not know of Her Majesty's departure. It would be an admission to the conspirators that the King feels his weakness, and would invite attack. For this reason she could not leave in the ordinary way. Fortunately, it is not difficult for Her Majesty to escape recognition. She is perhaps the one Queen in Europe whose published portraits would not make it impossible for her to go unknown through the cities of the Continent. Her prejudice against photographs has given her that immunity. She might walk through Paris unrecognized."

Benton looked narrowly at Von Ritz. "How much does she know of the truth?"

"Absolutely nothing. She has been persuaded to regard the truancy as a break in the routine of Court life, which—" Von Ritz hesitated, then went on doggedly—"which she finds distasteful. She does not even know that the Duke is free. That is as closely guarded a secret as the fact that he was being held under duress."

The soldier paused, then went on. "The King has told Her Majesty that he hopes to join her on your yacht within a few days. You will please encourage that fiction. In point of fact," with a gesture of despair, "if His Majesty were to leave now he would never return, and if he remains now he may never again leave. I must myself hasten back."

The two men went at some length over the details of the situation. It was agreed that the simple name of a town received by wireless should be a signal upon which the *Isis* would proceed with all possible haste to the place designated. If the necessity should arise for Karyl's leaving Galavia, he might in this way take refuge on the yacht. This, explained Von Ritz, was only the final precaution of preparing for every exigency. His Majesty was determined not to leave his city alive, until he could leave it in the full security of his established government.

The King also made another request. If Blanco could be spared and would consent to come to Puntal, his proven ability, together with his understanding of the language and the fact that he was not generally known in Puntal, would give him untold value. All the government's secret agents were either under suspicion of treason or too well known to the conspirators to be of great avail. If Blanco agreed to come, he might return with Von Ritz, or follow him at once and await instructions at his hotel, using care to avoid the semblance of open communication with the Palace.

On his return to the parlors, Cara presented Benton to her ladies-in-waiting, the Countess Fernandez and the Countess Jaurez, who were to travel as Miss Carstow's aunts.

When there is a three-quarter moon and an atmosphere as subtle as perfume; when the walls of the city lose their ragged lines and melt into soft shadow shapes, relieved here and there by lights which the waters mirror, night and the Bay of Naples are not bad. Then the small boats which bob alongside are filled with picturesque beggars raising huge bunches of violets on bamboo poles to the deck rails, and the mingling of singing voices with guitars sets it all to music.

On the forward deck Benton stood leaning on the rail and looking toward the city. At his side was Cara Carstow. She was silent, but she shook her head, and the man's solicitous scrutiny caught the deepening thought-furrow between her eyes, and the twitching of her fingers.

He bent forward and spoke softly. "Cara, what is it?" She looked up and smiled. "I was remembering that I stood just here, once before," she said.

"Do you think," he asked quietly, "that there has been a moment since then that I have not remembered it? That night you belonged to me and I to you."

"I guess," she said rather wearily, "we don't any of us belong to ourselves or to those we love most. We just belong to Fate."

"Cara!" He gripped the rail tightly and his words fell evenly. "Over there in America, you admitted to me that you loved me. That was when you were not yet Queen of Galavia." He brought himself up with a sudden halt. She looked up as frankly as a child.

"I didn't admit it," she said. "We only admit things against our will, don't we? I told you gladly."

"And now—!" He held his breath as he looked into her eyes.

"Now I am the Queen of a hideous little Kingdom," she shuddered. "It wouldn't do for me to say it now, would it?"

"Oh!" The man leaned again heavily on the rail. The monosyllable was eloquent. Impulsively she bent toward him, then caught herself. For a moment she looked out at the water undulating under the moon like mother-of-pearl on a waving fan. "But it was all right to say I loved you then," she went on reflectively, after a pause. "I had a perfect right then to tell you that I loved you better than all the small total of the world beside, and—" her voice faltered for a moment—"and," with a musical laugh, she illogically added, "I have nothing to take back of what I then said, though of course I can't ever say it again."

CHAPTER XXII

THE SENTRY BOX ANSWERS THE KING'S QUERY

Several days later, Blanco arrived in Puntal shortly after the lazy noon hour.

Out of disconnected fragments of fact and memory he had evolved a theory. It was a theory as yet immature and half-baked, but one upon which he resolved to act, trusting to the lucky outcome of subsequent events for the filling in of many gaps, and the making good of many deficiencies.

Among the shreds of fragmentary information which Manuel had previously stored away in his memory was the fact that one José Reebeler was a capitalist. This was not exclusive information. Every guide and casual acquaintance hastened to sing for the newcomer the saga of Reebeler's importance. One was informed that this magnate owned the three tourist hotels and their acres of vine-covered gardens; that he controlled the half-humorous pretense of a street-railway company and that even the huge, dominating rock upon which perched the pavilions and casino of the Strangers' Club was his property. Still more significant, to Blanco's reasoning, was the fact that Reebeler, though Puntal-born, was of British parentage and that over his house, in the *Ruo do Consilhiero*, floated both British and American flags, while the double coat-of-arms above his balcony proclaimed him the consular agent of both governments. Here, reasoned Blanco, was a man shielded behind the devices of two nations, neither of which was engaged in petty Mediterranean intrigue. He would be the last man in Puntal to challenge a suspicious glance from the Palace, yet as a man of moneyed enterprise his wish for concessions might well give a political coloring to his thoughts. Somewhere he had heard that the Strangers' Club aspired to the establishment of a gambling Mecca which should rival Monte Carlo in magnitude and that the present impediment was the frown of the government upon such a wholesale gambling enterprise. It was quite unlikely that the Delgado government would discourage a syndicate which could turn a munificent revenue into its taxing coffers.

Through a shaded courtyard where a small fountain tinkled, Blanco strolled to the Consular office and rapped on the door. He was conducted by a native servant to an inner room. Here, while a great blue-bottle fly droned and thumped, Reebeler, a heavy Briton with mild eyes, sprawled his length in a wicker chair and poured brandy and soda. First Blanco represented himself as an adoptive American, touring the world and interested in natural resources. When his host had exhausted the subject of the wine-grower's battle against the ravages of "*oidium Tuckeri*" and "*phyloxera*," Blanco picked up a stick of sealing-wax from the table and commenced toying with it in a manner of aimlessness. He struck match after match and melted pellet after pellet of wax, then absently he took from his pocket a gold seal-ring and made, with its shield, several impressions on the wax. Reebeler's eyes were half-closed as he gazed vacantly at the pigeons cooing and strutting in his courtyard.

"See, I have at last got a good impression." The Spaniard idly tossed over the scrap of paper upon which he had stamped a half-dozen of Louis Delgado's crests from the die of the Comptessa Astaride's ring.

The Consul took the fragment of paper with the manner of one forced by politeness to assume an interest in trivialities which bore him.

"See how clearly the device of His Grace stands out in the last impression," casually suggested Blanco, then with eyes narrowly bent on the other he saw the astonished start as his vis-a-vis realized what device had been imprinted on the paper. It was the sign for which he had played. When Reebeler's eyes came up questioningly to his own, he, too, was looking off through the raised window where the limp curtain barely trembled in the light breeze.

"The ring is interesting," suggested the Consul.

"The arms seem to be those of a family of Galavia which is connected with Royalty. Did you pick it up in a curio shop? If so, some servant must have stolen it."

Blanco stood up. "We waste time fencing, *Señor* Reebeler," he said, "His Grace, Louis Delgado, was held captive by the King until several days ago. He then escaped. That escape has been kept secret by the King. Only men in the Duke's confidence know of it. I am in the service of His Grace and I report to you. In these times we do not carry signed letters of introduction—those of us at least who are not protected behind the insignia of Consular office."

There was a long silence. Reebeler, under the influence of brandy and perplexity, breathed heavily. Blanco poured from a squat bottle and watched the soda bubble in the glass.

Finally the Consul inquired with a show of indifference: "Why do you assume that I know anything of this matter?"

Blanco laughed. "I have already told you that I come from His Grace. Naturally His Grace knew to whom to commend me. I have frankly given myself into your hands by declaring my sentiments. On the other hand, you decline a similar confidence. You are discreet." He waved his hand. "*Adios.*"

"Wait." The Consul stopped him at the door. He paused, cleared his throat and then abruptly suggested: "Suppose you return to-morrow at six."

The Spaniard bowed. "I only wish you to test me, *Señor.*"

That evening Blanco knew that he was being shadowed. The next day he had the same sense of being incessantly watched. This was a thing which he had expected and for which he was prepared. Promptly at six o'clock he returned to the *Rue do Consilhiero.*

He knew that his greatest danger lay in the possibility of communication by the conspirators with the Duke or the Countess, but he had been assured that Marie Astaride was in Cairo and it could safely be assumed that Delgado would return to Galavia only at the psychological moment. If either of these assumptions were false Louis would, of course, recognize the description of his kidnapper. The Countess would connect the episode of the ring with the former checkmating of her plans. At all events, he must chance those possibilities.

This time the Consulate was discreetly shut in by drawn jealousies. Within, beside Reebeler himself, were a number of men, all of whom narrowly scrutinized the newcomer. Those who were not in uniform carried themselves with a cocky smartness that belied their civilian clothes. The man from Cadiz returned their gaze with the same imperturbable steadiness and the same concealed wariness which he had employed when, in the *Plaza de Toros*, he awaited the charge of the bull.

For a time they allowed him to stand in silence under the embarrassing batteries of their eyes, then an elderly officer assumed the position of spokesman.

"If you are a spy your experience will be brief," he announced.

Blanco smiled.

"That is as it should be, *Señor.* Spies are not entitled to an old age."

"We are going to test you," continued the officer. "We have need of men of courage. If, as you claim, the Duke sent you, he must have done so because he regarded you as available. If you prove trustworthy, all right. If not, it is your misfortune, because in the place where we mean to use you you will have no opportunity to betray us, and a very excellent opportunity of meeting death. We cannot now communicate with His Grace for corroboration, so we shall let you prove yourself. You seem to bear no message from the Duke. That has the smell of suspicion."

"On the contrary," retorted the Spaniard, "the Duke believed that a man who was a stranger might prove of value. I was to take my instructions from you."

Blanco wondered vaguely what the future held for him. Evidently their acceptance of his services was to bear a close resemblance to imprisonment. He could see in the programme small opportunity to serve the King. His instructions had been to win into their confidence and do what he could.

Two weeks later, in the small garden giving off from the King's private apartments, and perched half-way up the buttressed side of the rock on which sat the Palace, Karyl impatiently awaited the coming of Colonel Von Ritz. Below he could hear a brass band in the Botanical Gardens and out in the bay a German war-ship, decorated for a dance, blazed like a set piece in a pyrotechnic display.

There was peace, summer, perfume, in the moonlit air and Karyl smiled ironically as he reflected that even the bodyguard so carefully selected by Von Ritz might at any moment enter the place and raise the shout of "Long live King Louis!"

Leaning over the parapet, he could see one of his fantastically uniformed soldiery pacing back and forth before a sentry-box, his musket jauntily shouldered, and a bayonet glinting at his belt. Karyl stood looking, and his lips curled skeptically as he wondered whether the man would repel or admit assassins.

Somewhat wearily the King turned and leaned on the stone coping of the outer wall. He was at one end where a shadow cloaked him, but he lighted a cigarette and the match that flared up threw an orange-red light on his face, showing eyes which were lusterless. For a few moments he held the match in his hollowed palms, coaxing its blaze in the breeze. Before it had burned out there came a sharp report and Karyl heard the spat of flattening lead on the masonry at his back. The echo rattled along the rocky side of the hill. One of the sentry-boxes had answered his unasked question of loyalty.

He waited. There was no rush of feet. No medley of anxiously inquiring voices. Others had heard the report, of course, yet no one hastened to inquire and investigate. The King, pacing farther back where his silhouette was less clearly defined, laughed again, very bitterly.

Finally Von Ritz came. "It seems that we can rely on no one," he said. "The Palace Guard had been picked from the few in whom I still believed. I had hoped there was a trustworthy remnant."

"One of them has just tried a shot at me with one of my own muskets." The King spoke impersonally as though the matter bore only on the psychic question of trusting men. "The spot is there on the wall." Then he added with bitter whimsicality: "It seems to me, Colonel, that we have either very poor marksmen in our service, or else we supply them with very poor rifles."

For a moment Von Ritz almost smiled. "I was passing the point as he touched the trigger, Your Majesty," he replied with calmness. "I will personally vouch for his future harmlessness."

The lighted door, at the same moment, framed the figure of an aide. "Your Majesty," he said with a bow, "Monsieur Jusseret prays a brief audience."

Karyl turned to Von Ritz, his brows arching interrogation. In answer the Colonel wheeled and addressed the officer, who waited statuesquely: "His Majesty will not receive Monsieur Jusseret. Any matters of interest to France will receive His Majesty's attention when they reach him through France's properly accredited ambassador."

Yet five minutes later, Jusseret, escorted by several officers in the Galavian uniform, entered the garden through the door of the King's private suite. At the monstrous insolence of this forbidden invasion of Karyl's privacy, Von Ritz stepped forward. His voice was even colder than usual with the chill of mortal fury.

"You have evidently misunderstood. The King declined to receive you—" he began.

Karyl turned his head and looked curiously on. The keen, dissipated eyes of the sub-rosa diplomat twinkled humorously. For a moment the thin lips twisted into a wry smile.

"The King is hardly in a position that warrants declining to receive me," he announced with an ironically ceremonious bow to Karyl. He was imperturbable and impeccable from his patent-leather pumps to the Legion of Honor ribbon in his lapel.

"I offer the King an opportunity to abdicate his throne—and retain his liberty. Not only do I offer him his liberty, but also such an income as will make the cafés of Paris possible, and the society of other gentlemen who are also—well, let us say retired Royalties. I do this in the capacity of a private friend of the Grand Duke Louis Delgado." His smile was bland, suave, undisturbed.

Von Ritz took a step forward.

"Escort Monsieur Jusseret to the Palace gates!" he commanded, his eyes blazing on the Galavian officers. "The persons of even secret Ambassadors are sacred—otherwise—" His voice failed him.

The officers cringed back under his glance, but stood supine and inactive.

Karyl waited with a cold smile on his lips. His face was pale but there was no touch of fear in the expression. For a brief psychological moment there was absolute silence, then the Frenchman spoke again. "Gentlemen, you are my prisoners." Turning to the Colonel, he added: "You have clung to the waning dynasty, Von Ritz, until it fell, but your sword may still find service in Galavia. I offer you the opportunity. We have often crossed wits. Now, for the first time, I win—and offer amnesty."

For a moment Von Ritz stood white and trembling with rage, then with his open hand he struck the smiling face that seemed to float tauntingly before his eyes, and drawing his sword, stepped between the King and the suddenly concentrated group of officers who moved frontward with a single accord, hands on swords. They spread from a group into a line, and the line quickly closed in a circle around the King and the one man who remained loyal.

Karyl was himself unarmed. He raised a restraining hand to Von Ritz's shoulder, but before he could speak his head sagged forward under the impact of some sudden shock—some blow from behind—and things went dark about him as he crumpled to his knees and fell.

Von Ritz, struggling desperately with a broken blade in his hand was slowly overwhelmed by seeming swarms of men. Like a tiger caught in a net, his ferocity gradually waned until, bleeding from scratch-wounds in a half-dozen places, he felt himself sinking into a haze. His useless sword-hilt fell with a clatter to the tiles. As his arms were pinioned by several of his captors, he was dreamily aware that music still floated up from the Botanical Gardens and the German man-of-war. Nearer at hand, Von Ritz heard—or perhaps dreamed through his stupor that he heard—a voice exclaiming: "Long live King Louis!"

There had been no noise which could have penetrated beyond the King's suite. Less than ten minutes had elapsed since the sentinel had been pacing below. Jusseret, passing unostentatiously out through the Palace gate, glanced at his watch and smiled. It had been excellently managed.

Later, Karyl recovered consciousness to find things little changed. He was lying on a leather couch in his own rooms. The windows on the small garden still stood open and the moon, riding farther down the west, bathed the outer world in shimmer of silver, but at each door stood a sentinel.

Karyl remembered that during Louis Delgado's recent captivity he had fared in precisely the same manner, neither better nor worse.

The King rose, still a trifle unsteady from the blow he had received, and went out into the garden. There was no effort on the part of the saluting soldier to halt him, and once outside he realized why this latitude was allowed him. In addition to the man at the door, a second walked back and forth by the outer wall. As Karyl stepped into the moonlight this man, himself in the shadow, saluted as his fellow had done.

"I have the honor to command the guard, Your Grace," said the man in a respectful voice. "It is by the order of His Majesty, King Louis." Something in the enunciation puzzled Karyl with a hint of the familiar.

"Why do you remain outside?" he asked.

"Over this wall, any comparatively agile man might make his way to the beach, if he succeeded in passing the muskets of the sentry-boxes—and there are boats at the water's edge," explained the soldier with a short laugh. "I am responsible for the guard, so I keep this post myself. I believe myself incorruptible and men with thrones at stake might make tempting offers."

Karyl smiled. "What would you regard as a tempting offer?" he suggested.

For answer the man came into the light and lifted his cap. The King looked into the dark eyes of Manuel Blanco. "I won into their confidence by the hardest," he explained in a lowered tone, "but after that, I had no opportunity to leave them or communicate with you. This was all I could do. As it is, I shall be recognized as soon as the Duke arrives."

Blanco raised his voice again in casual conversation and beckoned to the sentinel at the door. When the man approached the Spaniard pointed over the wall. "Do you see that rock? Is that a figure crouching behind its shelter?" he demanded. As the man leaned forward, Manuel suddenly struck him heavily at the back of the neck with a loose stone caught up from the masonry's coping. The soldier dropped without a sound.

"Now, Your Majesty, we must risk it down the rock," prompted the man from Cadiz, in hurried, low-pitched words. "Moments are invaluable.... It is only while I command the guard that there is a chance of your escape.... An officer may come at any instant on a round of inspection—my discovery as the Duke's kidnapper is a matter of minutes.... I have been watched and tested in a hundred ways; it was only to-day that I convinced them of my fanatic zeal."

Blanco hurriedly gave his cap and cape to the King, donning himself the blouse of Karyl's undress uniform. Then the two crept cautiously down the rifted face of the cliff, holding the shadow of the crevices. One sentry-box they passed safely, and finally they edged by the second unnoticed. They had negotiated the hundred feet of descent and stood pressed against the bottom, hugging the black shadow. They were waiting an opportunity to slip across a narrow sliver of intervening moonlight to the beach and the boat which lay at the water's edge.

Occasional lazy clouds drifted across the sky. The two refugees, goaded by the realization that every wasted second cut their desperate hope more and more to a vanishing point, watched the fleecy scraps of mist skim by the moon afar off without veiling its face. Then for a short moment a shred of silver-tipped cloud cut off the radiance. Blanco seized the King's arm in a wordless signal. Karyl and the bull-fighter raced across to the boat that lay at the water's edge. In a moment more it was afloat and they were at the oars. The moon emerged and at the same instant an outcry came from above. The musket of the man in the lower sentry-box barked with a blatant reverberation. One of the figures in the boat drooped forward and sagged limply over his oars. The other only redoubled his efforts. And then again, like the curtain of a theater, a cloud dropped downward and quenched the moon and the sea and the rock in impartial obscurity.

CHAPTER XXIII

"SCARABS OF A DEAD DYNASTY"

Since the anchor had been weighed at Naples, the days had passed uneventfully for the indolently cruising *Isis* with no word from Galavia. But at last the operator caught his call and made ready to receive. The message consisted of one word, and the word was "Cairo."

Cara, with no suspicion of what was transpiring in Puntal, beguiled by the spell of smooth seas and *dolce-far-niente* softness of sky, was once more the frank and charming companion of the American days.

The single word of the Marconigram had left the American in perplexity. Evidently either Karyl or Von Ritz was to meet them at Cairo. Probably Cairo instead of Alexandria had been designated because the King had taken into consideration the possible danger from the plague at the seaport. He told Cara only that Karyl would join the vacation party there and kept to himself the reservation that his coming probably meant disaster. Yet when they reached Cairo there was no news awaiting them.

It was the night of a confetti fête at Shephard's Hotel. Among the trees of the gardens were ropes of lights and the soft color-spots of Chinese lanterns. Branches glittered with incandescent fruit of brilliant colors. Flags hung between the fronds of the palms and the plumes of the acacias, and among the pleasure-seekers from East and West of Suez fell pelting showers of confetti.

After dinner Cara and the ladies of her party had withdrawn to their rooms to prepare for the gay warfare of the gardens. Benton, awaiting them in the rotunda, lounged on one of the low divans which circle the walls of the octagonal chamber, beneath carved lattices and Moorish panels; a cigarette between his fingers and a small cup of black coffee on the low tabouret at his elbow.

The place invited lazy ease, and Benton was as indolent among his cushions as the spirit of brooding Egypt, but his eyes, watching the stairs down which she would come, remained alert.

Hearing his name called in a voice which rang familiarly, he glanced up to recognize the smiling face of young Harcourt, his chance acquaintance of Capri. He set down the small Turkish cup and rose.

"Come back to the bar and fortify yourself against the thin red line of British soldiery out there in the gardens. You can get a ripping highball for eight *piastres*," laughed the newcomer. But Benton declined.

"I am waiting for ladies," he explained. "I'll see you again."

"Sure you will." Harcourt paused. "I dash up the Nile in the morning, going to do Karnak and Luxor—you know, the usual stunt. Been busy all day buying scarabs and mummied cats, but I want to see you sometime to-night. By the way, I've heard something—"

"All right. See you later." Benton spoke hurriedly, for he had caught the flash of a slender figure in white on the stairs.

In the war of the confetti, man makes war on woman and woman on man, while over the field reigns a universal and democratic acquaintanceship.

Cara was on vacation, and a child—bent on forgetting that to-morrow must come. It was characteristic of her that she should enter into the spirit of the occasion with all the abandon it suggested.

Benton stood by as she gradually gave ground before the attacks of a stout, gray-templed Briton, a General of the Army of Occupation. She fought gallantly, but he stood doggedly before her handfuls of confetti, shaking the paper chips out of his eyes and mustache like some invincible old St. Bernard, and her slender Mandarin-coated figure retreated slowly before his red and medal-decked jacket.

"Watch out!" cried Benton, who followed her retreat, forbidden by the rules of warfare from giving aid, other than counsel, "The British Army is putting you in a bad strategic position."

She had retreated across the flower-beds and stood with her back to the rim of the fountain. Her box of confetti was empty and Benton also was without ordnance supplies.

Young Harcourt suddenly stepped forward from the crowd.

"Here!" he cried with a smile of frank worship, as he tendered a fresh box of confetti. "Take this and remember Bunker Hill!"

The British officer bowed.

"I surrender," he said, "because you violate the rules of war. Your confetti is not deadly and your tactics are mediocre, but your eyes use lyddite."

Inside Cara went to her room to wrestle with the tiny chips of multi-colored paper that covered her and filled her hair. In the hall, Harcourt came again to Benton.

"By Jove, she is a wonder," he said. Then he slipped his arm through Benton's and led him aside. The American followed supinely.

"Benton, do you remember the talk we had about Romance?"

Benton looked quickly up to forestall any possible personality to which he might object, but Harcourt continued.

"Do you know that chap, Martin—he doesn't call himself Browne now—has turned up again? He's been here. Not ragged this time, but well groomed and in high feather. To-day he left to go back to Galavia."

"Back to Galavia?" Benton repeated the words in astonishment. "What do you mean?"

Harcourt laughed. "The scales have turned and his Grand Duke is to be King after all."

Benton seized the boy by the elbow and steered him into one of the empty writing-rooms.

"Now, for God's sake, what do you mean?" he demanded.

"That's all," replied the young tourist. "They've switched Kings. Oh, it was so quietly done that the people of the city of Puntal don't know yet it's happened. The King died suddenly and Louis will ascend his throne."

"The King died suddenly!" Benton echoed the words blankly. "I don't understand."

"Neither do I. But Martin said the King was taken prisoner and tried to escape. He was shot."

"How did Martin know?" asked Benton slowly, trying to realize the full import of the boy's chatter.

"The news hasn't reached here, generally speaking. He said that the King's death has not even been made public there, but the Countess Astaride has been stopping here. Martin himself was in her party and he helped her to decipher the news from the Duke's code-telegram." He paused. "However," he added, "that may not interest you. The story probably bored you at first, but having told you the original tale, I had to add the sequel. What I really wanted to ask you, is to present me to the wonderful American girl. You will, won't you?"

Benton's back was turned to the window. He wiped his forehead with his handkerchief and stared at nothing.

"You will, won't you?" repeated the boy.

"Oh, yes, of course," Benton replied mechanically. "I shall ask permission to do so."

Outside on the terraced veranda, where one sips tea and overlooks one of the most varied human tides that flows through any street of the world, Benton and Cara sat at a table near the edge—the man wondering how he could tell her. Fakirs with spangled shawls from Assouit, bead necklaces, ebony walking-sticks, scarabs and souvenir postcards jostled on the sidewalk to pass their wares over the railing. Fat Arab guides with red fezes and the noisy jargon of half-mastered French and English discussed to-morrow's journeys with industrious globe-trotters.

On the tiles squatted a juggler from India. Under his white turban his glittering, beady eyes appraised the generosity of his audience as he arranged his flat baskets, his live rabbits and his hooded cobras for an exhibition of mercenary magic.

Along the street, heralded with tom-toms, came a procession of lurching camels, jogging donkeys, rattling carriages, acrobats leading dog-faced apes and trailing Arabs in fezes—the pomp and pageantry of a pilgrim returning from Mecca. Motors, victorias, detachments of cavalry swept by in unbroken and spectacular show.

Benton sat stiffly with his jaw muscles tightly drawn and his eyes dazed, looking at the girl across the table.

She turned from the street, eyes still sparkling with the reflected variety of the picture that hodge-podged Occident and Orient, telescoping the dead ages with to-day.

"Oh, I love things so," she laughed. "I'm as foolish as a child about things that are new."

With another glance at the shifting tide, she added seriously: "And every silly Oriental of them all is free to go where he pleases—to do what he pleases. I would give everything for freedom, and they have it—and don't value it!"

Then she saw the hard strain of his face. Slowly her own eyes lost the glow of pleasurable interest and saddened with the realization of being barred back from life.

The man bent forward. His fingers tightened on the edge of the table with a clutch which drove the blood back under his nails. It was a hard fight to retain his self-control. His question broke from him in a low, almost savage voice.

"Cara!" he demanded. "Cara, is there any price too high to pay for happiness?"

"What do you mean?" The intensity of his eyes held hers, and for a moment she feared for his reason. Her own question was low and steadying, but he answered in an unnatural voice.

"I hardly know—perhaps I have less right to speak now than ever—perhaps more. I don't know, I only know that I love you—and that the world seems reeling."

Something caught in his throat.

"I'm a cur to talk of it now. I want to think of—of—something else. I ought to think only what a splendid sort he was—but I can realize only one thing—I love you."

"Only one thing," she repeated softly. Then as she looked again into the feverishly bright eyes under his scowl, the meaning which lay back of his words broke suddenly upon her.

"*Was*!" she echoed in startled comprehension. "*Was*!—did you say was?"

The man remained silent.

"You mean that—?" she said the three words very slowly and stopped, unable to go on.

"You mean—that—he—?" With a strong effort she added the one word, then gave up the effort to shape the question. Her hand closed convulsively.

Benton slowly nodded his head. The girl leaned forward toward him. Her lips parted, her eyes widened.

The next instant they were misty with tears. Not hypocritical tears for an unloved husband, but sincere tears for a generous friend.

"Delgado escaped," he explained simply. "Karyl was captured." Again he spoke in few words. It seemed that he could not manage long sentences. "Then he tried to escape," he added.

She pressed her fingers to her temples, and leaned forward, speaking rapidly in a half-whisper that sometimes broke.

"Oh, it's not fair! It's not fair! I want to think only how splendid he was—how unselfish—how brave! I want to think of him always as he deserves, lovingly, fondly—and I've got to remember forever how little I could give him in return!"

"Yes, I guess he was the whitest man—" Benton stopped, then blurted out like a boy. "Oh, what's the use of my sitting here eulogizing him. I guess he doesn't need my praises. I guess he can stand on his own record."

"It's monstrous!" she said, and then she, too, fell back on silence.

Suddenly she rose to her feet, carried one hand to her heart and swayed uncertainly for a moment, steadying herself with one hand on the table.

The man turned, following her half-hypnotic gaze, in time to see Colonel Von Ritz bending over her hand. With recognition, Benton started up, then his jaw dropped and, doubting his own sanity, he fell back into his chair and sat gazing with blank eyes.

At Von Ritz's elbow stood Pagratide.

Slowly Benton came to his feet, his ears ringing. Then as Karyl turned from the girl and held out his hand to him, the American heard, as one listening through the roaring of a fever, some question about affairs in Galavia.

He heard Karyl answer, and though the words seemed to come from somewhere beyond Port Said, he recognized that the former King tried to speak in a matter-of-fact voice.

"I have no Kingdom. Louis took it."

Karyl had held out his left hand. The right was bound down in a sling. But these things were all vague to Benton because it seemed that the pilgrim's tom-toms were beating inside his brain, and beating out of time. He could see that Karyl's eyes also were weary and lusterless.

Turning with an excuse for travel-stain to be removed, Karyl halted.

"Benton," he said. There he fell silent. "Benton," he said again, forcing himself to speak in a voice not far from the breaking point, "Blanco—Blanco is dead."

He turned on his heel and went into the hotel.

Blanco dead! For a moment Benton felt an insane desire to rush after Karyl and demand his life for Blanco's. Some delirious accusation that this man cost him every dear thing in life seemed fighting for expression and reprisal, then he realized that the *toreador* had won his way into Pagratide's affection as well as his own. Tears came to his eyes for an instant. He focused his gaze on a cigarette-shop across the street.

"Lady!"

A grinning Egyptian face, surmounted by a red fez, showed itself over the railing. The girl started violently and seemed for a moment on the edge of hysteria. She laughed unnaturally. Thus encouraged, the Bedouin's grin broadened until it radiated good-humor across the swarthy visage from cheek-bone to cheek-bone.

"Nice scarabs, lady! Only five *piastres*—only one shilling," he spieled. "Scarabs of a dead dynasty. *Très antique.*"

CHAPTER XXIV

IN WHICH KINGS AND COMMONERS DISCUSS LOVE

In the gardens of the hotel, the paths lay ankle-deep in scattered confetti. Already the scores of lights were going out and those that remained shone on the wreckage of an entertainment ended.

Cara had gone to her rooms. In his own, at a window commanding the garden, Benton sat in an attitude of lethargic dejection, staring down on the lingering illuminations. His brain still swirled. A dozen times he told himself that matters were precisely as they had been; that the developments of the evening had brought no change, save a momentary belief in a mistaken rumor and a few wild dreams. When he had waited in the rotunda for Cara, he had known Karyl to be living. He knew it now, yet it seemed as though his life-rival had died and come again to life. It seemed, too, as though his own prison doors had swung open, and while he stood on the free threshold had slammed inward upon him, sweeping him back, broken and bruised with their clanging momentum.

To-morrow he must go away.

Benton looked at his watch. It was after four o'clock.

Then a knock came on the door. Benton did not respond. He feared that young Harcourt, belated and flushed with brandy-acid-soda, might have seen the light of his transom and paused for gossip. The thought he could not endure. Again he heard and ignored the knock, then the door opened slowly, and turning his head, he recognized Karyl on his threshold.

Just at that moment the American could not have spoken. He had come to a point of pent-up emotion which can move only by breaking dams. He pointed to a chair, but Karyl shook his head.

For a while neither spoke. Karyl's hair was rumpled; his eyes darkly ringed, and the line of his lips close set. Benton glanced out of his window. Across the gardens the wall was growing blanker, as lighted panes fell dark. One window, which he knew was Cara's, still showed a parallelogram of light behind its drawn shade. Karyl in passing followed the glance. He, too, recognized the window.

At last the Galavian spoke.

"Can you spare me a half-hour?"

Benton nodded. He would have preferred any other time. He needed opportunity for self-collection.

Again Karyl spoke.

"Benton, I might as well be brief. There are two of us. In this world there is room for only one. One of us is an interloper."

The American felt the blood rush to his face; he felt it pound at the back of his eyeballs, at the base of his brain. An instinct of fury, which was only half-sane, flooded him. Red spots danced before his eyes. The other had spoken slowly, almost gently, yet he could read only challenge in the words, and the challenge was one he hungered to accept.

He made a tremendous effort for self-mastery and rose slowly, turning a white face on his visitor.

"You told me," he said, enunciating each word with distinct deliberateness, "that you would fight me, when your throne freed you. You begin promptly. I am here, but—"

"I think you misunderstand me," interrupted Karyl.

"But," went on Benton, ignoring the interruption, "neither of us is free to fight. If we were, Pagratide, you may guess how gladly I'd put it to the issue. Good God, man, what could I lose?"

"Wait," said the late King of Galavia. "I have come here to talk with you, Benton, in a way which is unspeakably hard. Can you not make the same effort to lay aside passion that I am making?"

The American turned and paced the floor.

For a moment more there was the same embarrassed silence between them, then the Galavian continued, measuring his words, speaking with desperately studied effort to eliminate the feeling that struggled to the surface.

"You love my wife."

"And shall," replied the American in the same calculated, colorless voice, "while I live."

"I, too," said Pagratide. "Therefore we must talk."

"Wait." Benton raised a hand. "If we are to talk at all along these lines, Pagratide, there is only one way in which it can be done."

"And that is what?"

"That each of us, throughout, talks with only one thought in mind: her happiness; that one strip aside all conventions and talk as two utterly naked souls might talk."

"Of course," said Karyl simply. "Otherwise I should not have suggested it."

"Then," began Benton, "up to this point we are agreed."

The King, despite his pallor, smiled.

"I'm afraid you still don't understand me. I haven't come to murder you, or to invite murder, Benton. It would not help."

"You have just said that one of us is an interloper. Presumably you have come to decide which one it is."

Karyl shook his head.

"Benton, that point has been decided. Not by you or me, but it is decided."

"I don't understand you," admitted the American.

His visitor studied the few remaining lights in the garden beneath.

"I am no longer a King. I am an outcast. If I ever had a claim before God, it passed with my Crown. I could hold her now only by brutality. I told you I would free her and fight for her, but I saw her eyes to-night.... Benton, it is I who am the interloper!"

No answer came to Benton's tongue. Pagratide did not seem to expect one. After a moment he went on, with the manner of one who had thought out what he was to say, and who compels himself to go through with the prepared recital.

"If there is no throne, I must eliminate myself.... But for the time being I have given Von Ritz my parole.... The game is not yet quite played out.... He and Cara agree that I must play it to the end. After that there will be time to remedy mistakes." He paused.

"Pagratide," said the American slowly, "you are talking wildly. At all events, while everything impossible has happened to us, I think we can, after all shake hands."

Karyl extended his own.

"I have spoken as I have," he went on, "because it was necessary to be frank. Meanwhile I must ask you to place me under yet another obligation. There is one safe place for her. Will you take us with you on the yacht, and cruise in unfrequented ports, until Von Ritz reports to me?"

"Where is Von Ritz?"

"Gone back to Alexandria. He still cherishes hopes of a restoration. He wishes to return to Galavia."

"Can he return safely?"

Karyl shrugged his shoulders. "His conduct can hardly be construed as a political offense. He will be under suspicion, but all Europe would resent any injury to Von Ritz."

"The *Isis* is, of course, at your command."

In the same rooms where Karyl and his father had often consulted with Von Ritz on affairs of state, Louis Delgado sat in conference with a foreigner, who had no acknowledged position in the councils of any government, yet whose mind and execution had affected many. The foreigner was Monsieur Jusseret.

"Why," began the new Monarch testily, "do you believe that there should be delay in proclaiming myself? I shall feel safer with the Crown actually upon my head."

The Frenchman sat reflectively silent, his slim fingers spread, tip to tip, his elbows on the arms of the chair in which he lounged.

"Your Majesty is not a fisherman?" he suavely inquired. Louis rose impatiently.

"You know that I have no interest in such sports. Why do you ask?"

"It is unfortunate," mused the Master Intriguer, "since if Your Majesty were, you would realize the inadvisability of an effort to land the game fish too abruptly when he takes the hook. Your Majesty, however, realizes that it is wiser to eat ripe fruit than green fruit."

The King poured himself a glass of wine, which he gulped down nervously.

"You speak in riddles—always in riddles. What is unripe? The blow is struck, I am in possession. What is to be gained by waiting?"

Jusseret raised his brows.

"What blow is struck, Your Majesty? You know and I know that you occupy the Palace. Europe in general supposes that you have been here for some time as the guest of Karyl. Europe does not yet officially know that Karyl has vacated the throne. The governments agreed to recognize you, but the governments relied upon your adequately disposing of your royal kinsman. Yet he is now at large."

The Pretender wheeled suddenly on the calm gentleman sitting indolently in his chair. The Pretender's face paled.

"Do you mean, Monsieur Jusseret, that after enticing me into this mad enterprise you now purpose to abandon me?" The coward's terror added excitement to the questioning voice.

Jusseret smiled.

"By no means," he assured. "But Your Majesty must now play your part. I merely counsel holding the reins of government lightly—as Regent—until it is logically advisable to grasp them tightly as King. Karyl escaped. The man shot proves to be an unknown who had changed coats with the King. Ostensibly, His late Majesty is traveling. You are his representative. Now, if His Majesty and the Queen should fail to return from their journeyings, your position would be stronger."

Louis sank into a chair, deeply agitated. "I fear this man Von Ritz more deeply than Karyl."

"Naturally," was Jusseret's dry comment. "But Your Majesty will leave Von Ritz alone. I also, should like to see him disposed of—but leave him alone, or you will incur Europe's displeasure."

"What shall I do?" The question came in a note of plaintive helplessness.

The Frenchman shrugged his shoulders.

"If you ask my counsel, I should say send for one Martin. He has been of some service. He is a man of action. He is called the English Jackal. I should suggest—" He paused.

"Yes, yes—you would suggest what?" eagerly prompted the new King.

"Really, Your Majesty, you should act more promptly on hints. Diplomats cannot diagram their suggestions. I should suggest that the English Jackal also travel, with the understanding that if he should return to Galavia after the death of the late King and Queen—and that shortly—he may expect certain titles and recognition at Court, but if he returns before their death, he need expect nothing." Jusseret lighted a cigarette.

The Pretender sat silent, frightened, vacillating.

"And," went on Jusseret calmly, "there was one other suggestion which I shall make, if Your Majesty will permit me the liberty."

"What?"

"Touching Your Majesty's marriage—"

"Yes—Marie is also in some hurry about that. What is the devilish haste? One can be married at any time."

Monsieur Jusseret rose and began drawing on his gloves.

"Of course if Your Majesty sees fit, a morganatic marriage with the Countess Astaride would be entirely advisable—but for the Queen of Galavia, Europe will insist on a stronger alliance; on a union with more royal blood."

Louis came to his feet in astonishment.

"You dare suggest that?" he exclaimed. "You, who have been her ally and used her aid!"

"Pardon me—I suggest nothing. I repeat to Your Majesty, as the very humble mouthpiece of France, the sentiment of the governments, without whose recognition your dynasty can hardly stand."

CHAPTER XXV

ABDUL SAID BEY EFFECTS A RESCUE

Martin, tall and aggressively British, from the black silk tassel on his red fez to the battered puttees and brown boots that had once come out of Bond Street, stood watching the *Isis* outlined against the opposite walls of the Yildiz Kiosk.

Few pleasure-craft call at Constantinople.

"If you had not, as usual, been so damned late"—he turned with a gesture of raw impatience to the heavy-faced *Osmanli* at his side—"I could have pointed them out to you on Galata Bridge. As it is, they have returned to the yacht."

"May Heaven never again thwart your wish with delay, Martin *Effendi*." The Turk spoke placidly, his oily voice soft as a benediction, "I was delayed by pigs, and sons of pigs! Your annoyance is my desolating sorrow, yet"—he waved his hand with a bland gesture—"I am but the servant of His Majesty, the Sultan—whom Allah preserve—and the official is frequently detained."

"What is done, is done. *Bismillah*—no matter!" The Englishman curbed his annoyance and spoke as one resigned. "What now remains is this: We must see them, and you must learn to recognize them. You understand?"

The other bowed in unperturbed assent.

"All Europeans," he suggested, "dine at the Pera Palace Hotel—it is the Mecca of their hunger."

To the white man's voice returned the ring of asperity. "And at the Pera Palace, we shall not only see, but be seen. Likewise unless we have a care in this enterprise, we shall not only eat, but be eaten. A man may stare at whom he chooses on Galata Bridge."

"When I dine in a public place"—the *Osmanli* smiled cunningly from the depths of small pig-like eyes—"I shield myself behind a screen. Thus may I observe unobserved."

The sun had set, but the yellow after-glow still lingered in the sky behind Stamboul as the two men stood looking toward Galata Bridge, where their quarry had escaped them, and across the Golden Horn.

A pyramid of domes, flanked by a pair of slender minarets, daintily proclaimed the Mosque Yeni-Djami against the fading amber. On Galata

Bridge itself, the day-long tide of medleyed life was thinning. Where there had been an eddying current of turbans and *tarbooshes*, bespeaking all the tribes and styles which foregather at the meeting place of two Continents and two seas, there were now only the belated few.

To the jaded imagination of Martin *Effendi* and his companion, Abdul Said *Bey*, the falling of night over the quadruple city, smothering more than a million souls under a single blanket of blackness, made no appeal. They were watching a yacht.

Over the Pera roofs swept flocks of crows to roost in their garden rookeries at the center of the town. Across the harbor water, now too gloomy to reveal its thousands of jelly-fish, drifted the complaining cries of the loons. Then as the occasional city lamps began to twinkle, making the darkness murkier by their inadequacy, there arose from the twisting ways of Pera, Galata and Stamboul the night howling of thirty thousand dogs.

At length Martin held up the dial of his watch to the uncertain light.

"I must be off," he announced. "Jusseret is waiting at the Pera Palace. Don't fail us at seven-thirty."

The tireless features of Abdul Said *Bey* once more shaped themselves into a deliberate smile. "Of a surety, *Effendi*. May your virtues ever find favor in the sight of Allah."

For a moment the pig-like eyes followed the well-knit figure of the Englishman as it went swinging along the street. Then the Turk turned and lost himself in the darkness.

The Pera Palace Hotel stands in the European quarter of the town. To its doors your steps are guided by a trail of shop signs in English, French, German and Greek, among which appear only occasional characters in the native Arabic.

Almost immediately after Cara, Pagratide and Benton had seated themselves in the dining-room that evening, Arab servants secluded a corner table, close to their own, behind *mushrabieh* screens. The party for whom this distinguished aloofness had been arranged made its entrance through an unseen door, but the voices indicated that several were at table there. The waiter who served this table apart might have testified that one was an Englishman, wearing in addition to European evening dress the native *tarboosh*, or fez. Also, that against his white shirt-front glittered the Star of Galavia. The second diner wore one of the many elaborate uniforms that signify Ottoman officialdom. His eyes were small and pig-like, and as he talked no feature or gesture at the table beyond escaped his appraising scrutiny.

There was one other behind the *mushrabieh* screens. The niceties of his dress were Parisian, punctilious, perfect. In his right lapel was the unostentatious button of the *Legion d'Honneur.*

The Englishman spoke. "Much of your story, *Monsieur* Jusseret, is familiar to me. It will, however, prove interesting *in toto*, I daresay, to our friend Abdul Said *Bey*, whom Allah preserve."

There was a murmur of compliment from the Turk, adding his assurance of interest, and the Frenchman took up the thread of his narrative.

"We supposed that Karyl was dead—the Throne of Galavia clear for Delgado. Alas, we were in error!" The speaker shook his head in deep regret, as, turning to Martin, he added:

"It was a pardonable mistake. Let us hope the announcement was merely premature." He lifted his wine-glass with the air of one proposing a toast. "It becomes our duty to make that statement true. *Messieurs*, our success!"

When the three glasses had been set down, the Englishman questioned: "How did it occur?"

In the smooth manner of an after-dinner narrative, Jusseret explained the occurrences of the night when he had brought his plans to an almost successful termination. He told his story with charm of recital, verve and humor, and gave it withal a touch of vivid realism, so that even his auditors, long since graduated from the stage where a tale of adventurous undertaking thrilled them, yet listened with profound interest.

With the salad Jusseret sighed regretfully.

"I rather plume myself on one quality of my work, *Monsieur* Martin. I rarely overlook an integral detail. I, however, find myself growing alarmingly faulty of judgment."

"Indeed!" The Englishman was not greatly engrossed in the autobiographical phases of Jusseret's diplomatic felonies.

"I regret to acknowledge it, but it is, alas, true. I reflected that the world would resent harsh treatment of a man like Von Ritz. He had committed no crime. We could not charge treason against a government not yet born. I opposed even exile. He immediately rejoined his fleeing King—and has since returned to Puntal, where one can only surmise what mischief he agitates. It may be as well to consider his future."

"And now," callously supplemented the Englishman, "our new King feels an uncertainty of tenure so long as the old King lives, and I am rushed after this refugee Monarch with brief instructions to dispose of him."

There was a certain eloquence in the shrug of Jusseret's shoulders. "*Messieurs*, we have wrecked Karyl's dynasty, but it still devolves upon us in workmanlike fashion to clear away the débris."

Martin leaned forward and put his query like an attorney cross-examining a witness.

"Where was this Queen when the King was taken?"

"That," replied Jusseret, "is a question to be put to Von Ritz or Karyl. It would appear that Von Ritz suspected the end and, wise as he is in the cards of diplomacy, resolved that should his King be taken, he would still hold his Queen in reserve. That Kingdom does not hold to the Salic Law—a Queen may reign! And so you see, my colleagues," he summarized, "we, representing the plans of Europe, find ourselves confronted with questions unanswered, and with matters yet to do."

Martin's voice was matter-of-fact. "After all," he observed, "what are the odds, where the King was or where the Queen was at a given time in the past, so long as we jolly well know where they are to-night?" Turning to the Sultan's officer, he spoke rapidly. "You understand what is expected?" He pointed one hand to the party from the yacht. "The man nearest us is the King who failed to remain dead. That failure is curable if you play your game." He paused. "The lady," he added, "has the misfortune to have been the Queen of Galavia. You understand, my brother?"

The Turk rose, pushing back his chair.

"Your words are illuminating." He spoke with a profound bow. "In serving you, I shall bring honor to my children, and my children's children." With the Turkish gesture of farewell, his fingers touching heart, lips and forehead, he betook himself backward to the door.

Two hours later, alighting from a rickety victoria by the landing-stage, Cara made her way between the two men, toward the waiting launch from the *Isis*. Filthy looking Arabs, to the number of a dozen, rose out of the shadows and crowded about the trio, pleading piteously for *backshish* in the name of Allah. The party found itself forced back towards the carriage, and Benton fingered the grip of the revolver in his pocket as the other hand held the girl's arm. At the same moment there was a sudden clamor of shouting and the patter of running feet. Then the throng of beggars dropped back under the pelting blows from heavy *naboots* in the hands of *kavasses*.

An instant later a stout Turk in official uniform broke through the confusion, shouting imprecations.

"Back, you children of swine!" he declaimed. "Back to your mires, you pigs! Do you dare to affront the great *Pashas*?" Then, turning obsequiously, he bowed with profound apology. "It is a bitter sorrow that you should be annoyed," he assured them, "but it is over."

"To whom have we the honor of expressing our thanks?" smiled Pagratide.

The *Osmanli* responded with a deprecating gesture of self-effacement.

"To one of the least of men," he said. "I am called Abdul Said *Bey*. I am the humble servant of His Majesty, the Sultan—whom Allah preserve."

As the launch put off, the elliptical figure of Abdul Said *Bey*, on the lowest step of the landing, speeded its departure with a gesture of ceremonious farewell—fingers sweeping heart, lips and forehead. "If you go to shop in Stamboul," he shouted after them, "have a care. The pigs will cheat you—all save Mohammed Abbas."

When the reflected lights of the launch shimmered in vague downward shafts at a distance, he turned and the scattered throng of beggars regathered to group themselves about him with no trace of fear.

"You will know them when you see them in the bazaars?" he demanded. "You shall be taught in time what is expected—likewise *bastinadoed* upon your bare soles if you fail. Now you have only to remember the faces of the Infidels. Go!" He swept out his hand and the Bedouins scattered like rats into a dozen dark places.

If the panorama of Constantinople fades from a lurid silhouette to a sooty monotone by night, it at least makes amends by day. Then the sun, shining out of a sky of intense blue, on water vividly green, catches the tiled color-chips of the sprawling town; glints on dome and minaret, and makes such a city as might be seen in a kaleidoscope.

Her insatiable appetite for beauty had brought Cara on deck early. The early shore-wind tossed unruly brown curls into her eyes and across the delicate pink of her cheeks.

When the yachtsman joined her, she read in his eyes that he had been long awake and was deeply troubled. In the shadow of the after-cabin she stopped him with a light touch on his arm.

"Now tell me," she demanded, "what is the matter?"

His voice was quiet. "There is nothing in my thoughts that you cannot read—so—" He lifted the eyes in question, half-despairing despite the smile he had schooled into them. "Why rehearse it all again?"

Her face clouded.

He turned his gaze on the single dome and four minarets of the Mosque of Suleyman.

"Besides," he added at length, speaking in a steady monotone, "I couldn't tell it without saying things that are forbidden."

When she spoke the dominant note in her voice was weariness.

"My life," she said, "is a miserable serial of calling on you and sending you away. Back there"—she waved her hand to the vague west—"it is summer—wonderful American summer! The woods are thick and green.... The big rocks by the creek are splotched yellow with the sun, and green with the moss.... I wonder who rides Spartan now, when the hounds are out!" She broke off suddenly, with a sobbing catch in her throat, then she shook her head sadly. "You see, you must go!" she added. "You will take my heart with you—but that is better than this."

She turned and led the way forward and for the length of the deck he walked at her side in silence.

As they halted he demanded, very low; "And you—?"

Her answering smile was pallid as she quoted, "'More than a little lonely'—" then, reverting to her old name for him, she laughed with counterfeited gayety—"as, Sir Gray Eyes, people must be—who try to be good."

CHAPTER XXVI

IN A CURIO SHOP IN STAMBOUL.

The *muezzin* had called the devout to their prayer-rugs for the third time that day, when the girl and the two men turned from the Stamboul end of Galata Bridge into the tawdry confusion of buildings which cluster about the Mosque Yeni-Djami. They were bound for the bazaars.

Along the twisting ways stretched the booths of native merchants stocked with the thousand fascinating trifles that the City of the Sultan markets to the journeying world. Everywhere the crowd surged and jostled.

On the side street where the shops are a trifle larger than their neighbors, one Mohammed Abbas keeps his curio bazaar. In such flowery Orientalism of appeal did he couch his plea for an inspection of his wares, that Cara was persuaded and turned into the shop. Cut off by pressure of the crowd, Pagratide, who was following, some paces back, caught a glimpse of her figure in the door and fought his way to her side, but Benton, having stopped to price a bracelet of antique silver set with turquoises, lost sight of them. The girl had become interested in a quaint, curved dagger thickly studded with semi-precious stones.

Mohammed Abbas urged her to see the rarer and choicer articles which he kept in an upper room. As they tailed, a half-dozen natives, swarthy and villainous of face, drifted into the shop to be promptly ordered out by the proprietor, who used for that purpose a vocabulary of scope and vividness. The ruffians retreated after a brief conversation in guttural Arabic, but not by the street door through which they had come. Instead, they left by a low-arched exit to the rear, concealed from view by the angle of the screening stairway. Abbas led his customers to an upper room which they found dark except where he lighted it as he went with hanging lamps. Its space was generous, broken here and there by piles of ebony furniture, inlaid with pearl; pieces of Saracenic armor, Damascened bucklers, and all the gear too large for the narrow confines below.

Half an hour's searching through the chaos of wares failed to reveal the choice daggers which Mohammed wished them to see, and with many apologies for added annoyance he begged *Monsieur* and *Madame* to mount yet another flight, and visit yet another store-room. At the head of these stairs they encountered absolute darkness and the shopman, with his ever-ready apologies, paused again to light lamps.

As Pagratide's pupils accustomed themselves to the murk he realized that this last room was bare except for tapestries hung flat against the wall, and that at its farther side narrow slits of light showed along the sills of two doors. Turning, he noted the darker shadow of some recess in the wall, immediately to his left.

Suddenly Mohammed Abbas closed the door upon the stairs, and sharply clapped his hands. In all lands where Allah is worshiped, clapping of the hands is a signal of summons. Thrusting his hand into the pocket where he had stored an automatic pistol, Karyl found it empty, and remembered that on the stairway the merchant had apologized for jostling him. Then simultaneously the two opposite doors opened and framed against their light a momentary picture of crowding Arabs.

Outside, Benton had been searching. First he had felt only annoyance for a chance separation, but when ten minutes of futile wandering had lengthened to fifteen, annoyance gave way to fear, and fear to panic. A dozen tragic stories of mysterious disappearances in Stamboul crowded like nightmares upon his memory. At last, standing bewildered in the street, he caught sight of a familiar figure; a figure that filled him with astonishment and delight.

Colonel Von Ritz had left Cairo to return to Puntal. Now here he was in a crooked Stamboul street, appearing without warning, but with his almost uncanny faculty for being at the right spot when needed. He shouldered his way to the side of the officer.

Though the two men had parted several weeks before, the Galavian greeted the other only with a formal bow, and an abrupt question. "Where are they?"

"I have lost them," replied Benton. He rapidly sketched the events of the last half-hour, and confessed his own apprehensions.

With evidence of neither anxiety nor interest, Von Ritz listened, and replied with a second question. "Have you seen Martin?"

Benton gave a palpable start. "Martin!" he ejaculated. "Is Martin in Constantinople?"

For reply Von Ritz permitted himself the rare indulgence of a smile.

"Martin is here," he said briefly.

"And you—?"

As he spoke the figure of Martin himself emerged from a shop a few paces ahead, and without a backward glance cut diagonally across the narrow street to disappear into the doorway of the curio shop which is kept by Mohammed Abbas.

When, after being cut off and delayed for some minutes by a passing donkey train, Von Ritz and Benton entered the place, they found it empty except for a native salesman, but as the Galavian paused to make a trivial purchase his listening ear caught a sound above. Without hesitation, he wheeled and mounted the stairs with Benton close at his heels. Behind him the shop-clerk stood irresolute—taken aback, with a vague consciousness that he should have devised a way to stop this gigantic Infidel. Assuredly the master would be angry. Orders had been explicitly given to allow no one to climb those steps to-day without permission.

While Cara and Karyl had been on the second floor, a heavy *Osmanli*, wearing the Sultan's uniform, had stood in the center of the room above, looking about with keen, pig-like eyes, as he gave rapid commands to a half dozen Arabs of villainous visage.

"You, Sayed Ayoub," he ordered, "take your pig of a self and others like unto you into that doorway by the stairs. Remain until you hear men enter from these two doors, facing the Infidel dogs. Then come upon them from behind. The man is to be bound, and when evening comes—but that is later! Still, if he resists too much—" The speaker shrugged his heavy shoulders and made a certain gesture.

"And the woman? What of her?" The question came from a gigantic Bedouin whose evil countenance was made the more sinister by one closed and empty eye-socket.

Abdul Said *Bey* nodded. "She is to be tenderly handled," he enjoined. "She, also, must disappear, but that shall be my care. My harem is as silent as the Bosphorus."

There were steps on the stairs, and instantaneously the room emptied itself and became silently dark.

When Karyl heard the hand-clapping of the decoy shopman, and saw the responding ruffians in the opposite doors, he swiftly thrust the girl into the spot of blacker shadow at his back, and seized the wrist of Mohammed Abbas with a force and suddenness that wrung from him a piteous wail.

Keeping the Turk before him, he backed toward the shadowed recess, with the one idea of shielding Cara. But the darker spot was the door behind which Sayed Ayoub lay in ambuscade, and as Karyl reached it, it swung open, showing them against a background as bright as though they were painted on yellow canvas.

With his free arm he swept Cara into the doorway, wheeling quickly in front of her, and sent Mohammed Abbas lurching forward into the faces of the assailants led by Sayed Ayoub. Instantly, however, his arms were pinioned from behind by the reënforcements, and as he frantically struggled to turn his face, in an effort to see the girl, some thick fabric fell over his head, covering mouth and eyes, and he went down stifled and garroted into insensibility.

Seeing the man overwhelmed and dragged through the door, Cara stood rigidly upright, white in the intensity of voiceless outrage, until the gigantic brute with one sightless eye and a greasy *tarboosh* reached out his grimy hand and seized her. Then she sickened at the profaning shock of his touch, and fell unconscious.

A few moments later the "English Jackal" stood nonchalantly looking down at the bound figure of the former King lying on the floor, shoulders propped against the wall, head wrapped in a richly embroidered shawl from Persia. Lamps had been kindled. The head wrappings had already been somewhat loosened and Karyl was stirring with the indication of returning consciousness.

"Oh, damn it!" remarked Martin in disgust. "He doesn't need to be both trussed up and gagged, you know. He's quite safe. Take off the head cloths."

He stuffed tobacco into his blunt bull-dog pipe as he supervised the undoing of the smothering fabric and complacently looked at his prisoner.

Freed from the bandage, and drinking in again reviving breaths, Karyl awoke to the sense of his surroundings. His eyes at once swept the place for Cara, but he saw only the closed door of the room where she was detained.

Martin looked down and as their eyes met he casually nodded.

"Sorry to inconvenience you," he commented affably, "but this is politics, you know. I happen to work for the other chap, King Louis." As an afterthought he added: "And the other chap thinks that you are, to put it quite civilly, unnecessary."

He smoked meditatively, while Karyl, without reply, scowled up into his face. The sense of futility left Pagratide silent. He lay insanely furious like a trapped wolf, able only to glare.

Suddenly the complacency deserted the Englishman's features, for a startled expression. With a violent malediction he bent forward listening.

Karyl's ears also caught the sound of feet on the stairs, immediately followed by a crash upon the door.

Martin drew a heavy revolver from a holster under his coat, and his voice ripped out orders with the sharp decision which had survived the days when he wore a British uniform. "Here, you beggars," he shouted, "to that door!"

As the Bedouins swarmed forward there came a second crash under which the panels fell in, precipitating Von Ritz and Benton into a fierce swarm of human hornets.

Falling desperately upon the newcomers with swords, knives and *naboots*, the bravos afforded them no time to take breath after their climb of the stairs.

Martin, standing with his pipe clamped between his teeth, took no part in the onslaught. He cast a glance at the turmoil, then deliberately cocked his weapon and leveled it at the breast of his captive.

Karyl realized that the Jackal was not to be led away from his single purpose: that of execution. If he himself were to speak to his rescuers, he must do it quickly. He raised his voice.

"Von Ritz! To that door!" he shouted loudly, but the Galavian and his companion, fighting desperately to hold their own, with the shouts and clamor of the struggling Moslems in their ears, did not hear, and the Englishman only smiled.

"They are quite busy, you know," he drawled in a half-apologetic tone. "Give them a bit of time."

Von Ritz was fighting with the blade of his sword-cane, while Benton, too closely pressed to make use of his pistol, was relying upon his fists. Indeed, the two white men owed their lives to the crowding which made effective fighting impossible on either side.

At last the Turks gave back a few steps for a fresh rush and Benton, taking instant advantage of the widened space, fired into the crowd. They turned in terror at the first report and went stampeding to the several doors. Then for the first time the rescuers caught sight of the Englishman standing guard over the bound figure on the floor.

With the grim smile of one who, recognizing the end, neither flinches nor dallies, Martin fired two shots from his leveled revolver.

A half-second too late Benton's magazine pistol ripped out in a frenzied series of spats. The Englishman swayed slightly, his face crimson with blood, then, propping himself weakly against the wall, he fired one ineffectual shot in reply. Slowly wilting at waist and knees, his figure slipped to the floor and lay shapelessly huddled near that of Karyl. The stench of powder filled the room. Twisting spirals of smoke curled ceilingward.

Von Ritz and Benton, kneeling at the King's side, raised him from the floor. The wounded man attempted to speak. His eyes turned inquiringly toward the door of the other room. Benton caught the questioning look and nodded his head. Then Karyl settled back against the officer's supporting shoulder after the fashion of a reassured child.

"The King is dead," said Colonel Von Ritz quietly. There was something very pathetic in the steady despair of his voice.

A door opened, and several Bedouins retreated shame-faced and cowed before a heavy Turk who wore the Sultan's uniform. His small, pig-like eyes blazed with terrifying wrath. Looking about the room for a moment, he volcanically reviled them.

"You dogs! You pigs! You serpents!" he shrieked. "Your hearts shall be thrown to the buzzards! Your children dishonored! You have dared to attack the foreign *Pashas*, and you—Mohammed Abbas—!" The shopkeeper fell trembling to his knees. "Your filthy shop shall be pulled down about your ears. You make it a trap—your feet shall be *bastinadoed* until you are a cripple for life!" Then his rage choked him, and, wheeling, he walked over to Benton, contemptuously kicking the prostrate body of Martin *Effendi* as he went.

From every pore Abdul Said *Bey* exuded sympathy and commiseration. Scenting liberal *backshish*, he promised absolute secrecy for the affair, coupled with soothing assurances of private vengeance upon the surviving miscreants. Also, he bewailed the disgrace which had fallen upon the Empire by reason of such infamy. He presumed that the foreign gentlemen preferred secret punishment of the malefactors to a public sensation. It should be so.

In his anxiety for Cara, Benton left Von Ritz to adjust matters with the Turk, who with profound courtesy and amazing promptness had closed carriages at a rear door, and caused his *kavasses* to clear the alley-way of prying eyes.

When the American reached the room where Cara had been left it was deserted by the assassin's guards. With a sudden stopping of his heart, he saw her lying apparently lifeless on a stacked-up pile of rugs. In a terror that he scarcely dared to investigate, he laid his ear hesitantly to her breast, then, reassured, he gave thanks for the anesthetic of unconsciousness with which nature had blinded her to the tragedy beyond the closed door.

Two curtained carriages drove across Galata Bridge and in the mysterious quiet of Stamboul there was no ripple on the surface of affairs as other tourists haggled over a few *piastres* in the curio shops of the bazaar.

CHAPTER XXVII

BENTON SAYS GOOD-BY

Louis Delgado awaited Jusseret in an agony of doubt and fear.

The Frenchman was late. A dispatch from the frontier had announced his coming, but to the anxiety of Delgado delays seemed numberless and interminable.

At last an aide ushered him into the apartment where the new Monarch waited, his inevitable glass of Pernod and anisette twisting in his fingers. Jusseret bowed.

"Where is Martin?" inquired the King.

"Dead," said the newcomer briefly. The Pretender paled palpably. Evidently the plan had gone awry. Fear always stood near the fore, ready to rush out upon Delgado's timid spirit.

"And being dead," resumed the Frenchman, "he is much safer."

Louis gave a half-shuddering sigh of relief. He had none of that righteous horror of crime which makes the face of murder hideous, but in its place he had all the terrors of the weak, and playing with life and death gave him over to panic.

"I should suggest an announcement that King Karyl had fled for a time from the cares of State and was traveling as a private gentleman in strictest incognito, when sudden death overtook him. There need be no hint of violence. There must be a State funeral."

"Where is the body?" objected Louis.

Jusseret shrugged his shoulders.

"That I cannot say. I can, however, assure you that it is quite lifeless. Since the death occurred some days ago the lying in State may be dispensed with. A closed casket is sufficient."

"And his Queen?"

"That point is left unguarded, but from intimations I have received, I believe the Queen will be satisfied with private life. If you announce her abdication, she will hardly contradict you."

"And Von Ritz?" persisted Louis, with the manner of one who wishes all the ghosts which terrify him laid by someone stronger and less afraid of ghosts than himself.

"Leave Von Ritz to me. He is no fool. Von Ritz knows who instigated the murder of the King, but he is without proof. The thing happened far beyond the borders of Galavia."

Louis rose unsteadily from his chair.

"Jusseret," he began, "this interview with Marie still confronts me and I dread it. Would it not be better for you to explain to her? You could persuade her that Kings are not free in these matters, that crowned heads from antiquity to Napoleon have been compelled to obey the dictates of State."

The Frenchman stiffened.

"Your Majesty," he observed, "it is impossible. Your attachment for the Countess Astaride is a personal matter. I am concerned only in affairs of State. I must even require of you, in respect to that confidence which obtains between gentlemen, that you shall in no wise intimate that this suggestion came from me."

The new incumbent, who had brought to the Throne of Galavia all the libertine's irresoluteness, paced the floor in perplexed distress. He feared Jusseret. He dared not anger or disobey him. It appeared that being a King was not what he had conceived it, as he sat under the chestnut trees of the Paris boulevards and listened to the band.

When Jusseret had left him to his thoughts he paused three times with a tremulous finger on the call-bell, unable to command the courage required to send a message to the Countess Astaride. Finally he succeeded and five minutes later stood shamefacedly in the presence of the woman who had made him King. She was more than usually beautiful, and as always her beauty and personality dominated him, swayed his senses like music. It was so easy to slip into the impetuous attitude of the lover; so difficult to maintain the austere one of the Monarch.

Delgado nerved himself and began.

How he said it or what he said, he did not himself know when the words had been spoken. He rushed through the speech he had prepared like a frightened child at recitation and waited for the outburst of her anger. He waited in vain.

Marie Astaride had plotted, had consented to every infamy which had been suggested as necessary to bring the man she loved to the Crown.

Now she was silent.

The man looked up when he had waited a seeming century for the expected torrent of reproach.

She was standing supporting herself upon her downward stretched arms, her hands resting on the table. Her face was pallid and her magnificent figure rigid. The scarlet fullness of her lips had gone bloodless. Her eyes were stupefied.

At length she straightened herself, let go her support upon the table and went slowly like a sleep-walker from the room. She had not spoken. She had not said good-by, but Louis Delgado knew that she had walked out of his life.

That evening Monsieur Jusseret of the French *Cabinet Noir* met, as if by chance, young Lieutenant Lapas, who was now high in the favor of the new government. Jusseret knew that the lure which had drawn young Lapas away from the confidence of Karyl to the uncertain standard of Delgado had been the influence of the Countess Astaride. He knew that Lapas loved her hopelessly, willing even in her name to serve the greater man who loved her more successfully. His attachment was that of the boy for the woman who is mistress of all the mature arts of charm. This love could be turned into the fanatic's zeal; this boy could be led to the extreme of martyrdom, if the strings of his characterless nature were played upon with a skill sufficiently consummate. Jusseret knew also a number of other things. He knew that whereas he had, to all seeming, brought a difficult task to completion, he was in reality not yet half through. His own vision went farther into the future, and recognized in the present only a mile-post far from the ultimate.

He led Lapas to his own rooms. He was leaving for Paris the following morning, he explained, and wished a brief conference.

Jusseret could, when occasion demanded, be not only calm and self-sufficient, but also emotional. Now he was emotional.

"Rarely, indeed," he began, "do I permit personal indignation to excite me. But this is so unspeakable that I wished to talk to you. You enjoy the confidence of the Countess Astaride?"

"Only in a humble way," confessed young Lapas.

"But you are her friend? If she were wronged and had no other defender, you would assume her cause?"

"With my life," protested the officer, fervently.

"This matter," said Jusseret dubiously, "might cost you your life. Possibly I should not tell you. As a politician I can have nothing to do with it, but as a man, I wish I were myself free to act."

"Who has offended the Countess?" demanded Lapas hotly.

"Offended, my young friend! This is not an offense. It is the gravest indignity that can be shown a woman. It is an insult to which a man must either blind himself—or punish with such means as can ignore personal peril."

"For God's sake," insisted the other, "explain yourself."

"Louis Delgado," began Jusseret quietly, "accepted this woman's love: enjoyed it to the full. He sat and dreamed over his absinthe futile dreams of power. He was too weak to strike a blow—too weak to raise a hand. Then she took up his cause; intrigued, enlisted our interests, raised his supine and powerless ambitions to a throne. There he abandons her at the foot of the stairs by which he mounted; and refuses her his Crown. He talks now of a more Royal alliance." Jusseret spread his hands in a gesture of disgust.

Lapas rose tensely from his chair. The veins on his temples stood out corded and deep-lined.

"This cannot be true, sir," he argued. "There must be some error. You wrong the King."

"Am I the man to wrong Louis?" questioned the Frenchman. "You have only to wait and see for yourself. The matter rests with you. She and I have put Louis on the throne. So much I did as the servant of my government. What I say to you I say as a man, and I had rather behold all my work undone than to stand by and see it bear such fruit. Adieu."

He rose slowly and took his departure. Outside, he smiled.

"I fancy," he told himself, "he will go to the Countess. I fancy she will corroborate me—and then—!" He dismissed the matter with his habitual shrug.

Two weeks had passed since the tragedy in Stamboul, and the *Isis* cruised aimlessly westward. The Mediterranean stretched to the horizon, so placid that the froth from the wake washed languidly, almost lifelessly, on the surface, and a single cloud hung stationary in the softer blue of the sky. Wrapped in a steamer rug, her figure, more slender in the simple lines of her black gown, Cara sat gazing toward the receding coast-line of Malta. So she had spent most of the hours since they had weighed anchor at Constantinople. On the deck at her feet sat Benton.

At Piræus Von Ritz had secured a copy of the *Figaro* several days old, and the men had read its report of the Regency of Louis in Puntal. Then the yacht had called at Malta where the gray fortresses of Valetta frown out to sea, and Von Ritz had once more gone in quest of news.

That had been yesterday. By common consent the two men refrained from allusions to State matters in the girl's presence. Now the former adviser of the King uneasily paced the deck. Over his usually sphinx-like face brooded the troubled expression of one who confronts an unwelcome necessity. Suddenly he halted before the girl's deck-chair, and, schooling his voice with an apparent effort, spoke in his old-time even modulation, but for once he found it difficult to meet the eyes of the person he addressed.

"We have heretofore not spoken of things which we would all give many years of life to forget," he began. Then he added with feeling: "Only the sternest necessity could force me to do so now."

As he paused for permission to continue, the girl raised her eyes with a sad smile that had grown habitual.

"I have come," said Von Ritz, "to stand for an implacable Nemesis to you, and yet I should wish to be identified only with happiness in your thoughts. To me one thing always comes first. The House of Galavia is my gospel; has been my gospel since Karyl's father mounted its throne." He paused and added gravely: "Louis Delgado has reaped his reward—he is dead."

Benton's voice broke out in an explosive "Thank God!"

Von Ritz stood a moment silent, then, dropping to one knee, he took the fingers which fell listlessly over the arm of Cara's steamer-chair and raised them to his lips.

"Your Majesty is Queen of Galavia."

The American came to his feet, his hands clenched, but with quick self-mastery he stood back, breathing heavily.

Cara sat for a moment only half-comprehending, then with a low moan she leaned forward and covered her face with both hands.

"Forgive me," said Von Ritz. "I *am* your Nemesis."

Benton moved over silently and knelt beside her chair. Neither spoke, but at last she raised her face and sat looking out at the water, then slowly one hand came out gropingly toward the American and both of his own closed over it. Von Ritz stood waiting.

When finally she spoke, her voice was almost childlike, full of pleading.

"I thought," she said, "that all that was over. I had thought that whatever is left of life belonged just to me—for my very own. I thought I could take it away and try to mend it."

Von Ritz turned his head and his eyes traveled northward and westward, where, somewhere beyond the horizon, lay his country.

"Galavia needs you," he said with grave simplicity. "Unless you come to her aid there must be ruin and dismemberment. You will save your country."

But his words appeared to convert all her crushed and pathetic misery into anger. "It is not my country!" she replied almost fiercely. "To me it means only—"

Von Ritz raised his hand supplicatingly. "It is my country," he said sadly, "and—your duty. Its fate is in your hands."

The girl rose, swayed slightly, and putting out one hand for support, stood with her black-gowned figure sketched slenderly against the white of the cabin wall, her eyes irresolute and distressed.

"I must have time to think," she begged. "Will you leave me?" Von Ritz bowed and retired.

She dropped exhaustedly into the chair again and for a long while sat silent. Finally she turned toward the man who, kneeling by her side, waited for her decision through what seemed decades of suspense, and her hands went out gropingly again toward him.

"Dear," she said in a voice hardly more than a whisper, "whatever I do—whatever I decide—always and always I love you!" Impulsively her fingers clutched at his, which rested clenched on her arm-chair.

"You must go!" she said, after a long while. "With you here there is nothing else in the world. I can see only you." With a catch in her voice she rushed on. "You must not only go, but I must not know where you go. I must not be able to call you back. You must give me your word of honor."

He attempted to speak, but she tightened her hold on his hands and her hurried utterance checked his words.

"No!" she said. "Listen! This time I decide forever. I must decide alone. You must not only be out of my sight, but beyond recall. Three months from to-day I shall write to you, but until then I must not know your address. Three months from to-day you may be at 'Idle Times,' where I first told you I loved you ... where we told each other ... if you still wish to be. Then, if I decide that I am free, you will find my letter there. If I'm not free, I had better not even write. I couldn't write without calling you back. If I have to decide that way—" She broke off with a shudder. "Oh, you must go—Dear!—you must go quickly—! It is the only way you can help me."

A half-hour later, Benton turned to the approaching Von Ritz.

"Colonel," he said steadily, "I sail for San Francisco by way of Suez from the first port we reach. You will favor me by accepting the *Isis* as long as Her Majesty can use it."

Von Ritz met his eyes in silence and held out his hand.

CHAPTER XXVIII

JUSSERET MAKES A REPORT

In Paris a small party of gentlemen, among whom were represented all the national types of Southern Europe, were engaged in an informal discussion of very formal affairs. They occupied a private suite in the Hotel Ritz overlooking the column of the *Place Vendome.* Upon a table swept clean of draperies and bric-a-brac lay an outstretched map of the Mediterranean littoral, whereon a small peninsula had been marked with certain experimental and revised boundaries in red and blue and black. The atmosphere was thick with the smoke from cigars and cigarettes, and through the veneering amenities of much courtesy the gentlemen of Europe's *Cabinets Noirs* wrangled with insistence. Finally Monsieur Jusseret took the floor, and the others dropped respectfully into an attitude of listening.

"It is hardly necessary," he began, "to discuss what has been done in Galavia. That is long since a stale story. Our governments, acting in concert, made it possible to remove Karyl and crown Louis." He smiled quietly. "You know how short a reign Louis enjoyed before death claimed him. Perhaps you do not know that his death was not unforeseen by me."

There was an outburst of exclamations under which France's representative remained unmoved.

"Our object," he explained coldly, "was the disruption of Galavia's integrity. In reducing this Kingdom to a province, the supplanting of Karyl with Louis was essential only as an initial step. The instability of that government had to be demonstrated to the world by more continuous disorders. It was necessary to show that the Kingdom had become incapable of self-rule. It followed that the removal of Louis was equally natural—and imperative."

Don Alphonso Rodriguez, bearing the secret credentials of Spain, came to his feet with the hauteur of offended dignity.

"My government" he said, with austere deliberation, "had the right to know what matters were being transacted. France appears to have assumed exclusive control. Is it too late to inquire of France"—he bent a chilling frown upon the smiling Jusseret—"what she now purposes? It appears that Spain knew no more than the newspapers. Spain also believed that Louis died by his own hand, and artlessly assumed the motive of disappointment in his love for Marie Astaride. We believed we were being frankly informed."

The more accomplished diplomat lifted brows and hands in a deprecating gesture. "*Mon ami*," he responded with suavity, "you flatter me. What I have done is nothing. I have only paved the way. Quite possibly Louis did kill himself. If so it was a meritorious act, but whether he did so or whether some mad young officer, infatuated and jealous, was the real author of the result, the result stands—and meets our requirements. France does not care what flag flies over the Governor-General's Palace in Puntal, provided it be the flag of a nation in concert with France. France suggests that the Governor-General should be a Galavian, and points to the one man conspicuously capable—who happens to be," he added with an amused laugh, "my particular enemy."

"You mean Von Ritz?" The question came from Italy's delegate.

Jusseret bowed his head. "Von Ritz," he affirmed.

Don Alphonso Rodriguez laughed with a note of incredulity. "And how do you propose," he demanded, "to persuade this loyal adviser of Karyl to accept a deputyship at the hands of Karyl's enemies?"

Again Jusseret smiled. "It will be Von Ritz or a foreigner," he explained. "We must convince him that his beloved Kingdom can henceforth be only a province in any event—that it may prosper under his guidance or suffer under a more oppressive hand. That done, his patriotism will prove our ally. We have only to convince him that no member of Karyl's house can reign and live—and that it must be himself or an alien."

"It would have been as easy," demurred the Portuguese delegate, "to have persuaded Von Ritz that Karyl himself should abdicate."

Jusseret felt the hostility of the other members. In spite of the realization, or perhaps because of it, he glanced from face to face with unruffled urbanity.

"*Messieurs*," he suggested, "you overlook the hypotheses—and in reaching conclusions hypotheses are serviceable. You, gentlemen," he continued blandly, "regarded the initial steps as impracticable. What I volunteered to do, I have so far done. We have one object. The insatiate ambition of that nation, which we need not name, must not gain additional Mediterranean foothold. Spain or Portugal, it is one to us, may decide the matter of suzerainty between themselves."

"How do you mean to persuade Von Ritz?" insisted Don Alphonso.

"In the young Queen, who is the sole eligible candidate for the Throne, we have at heart an unwilling heir. Von Ritz distrusts France. Let the suggestion come from Portugal, a friend who can speak persuasively—and convincingly. Let him see the inevitable result unless he consents. Let all which we have done be denounced. Lead him to believe that he holds as steward"—Jusseret raised his hands as he concluded—"for Karyl's heir, if there should be one. These things are mere details."

Benton worked his way slowly to San Francisco through the Far East. It is not difficult to avoid newspapers between Ismaïlia and Manila, and with the dogged determination to let the day set by Cara answer all questions of his future, he had neither sought nor received tidings from Galavia.

He had not permitted himself great indulgence in hope. The past months had brought too many disappointments, and he knew that they had all been but episodes leading up to the climax which must come with the day when he inquired for a letter at "Idle Times."

He dreaded a return to "Idle Times" before the day set for his inquiry. Bristow's place stood for too much of memory, and the inevitable questions of his friend loomed before him, as the trifle which a man who has stood much more than trifles cannot bring himself to face. Yet there was no danger of his being late. That time was the one fixed point on the calendar of his future. One day before his three months had come to an end, he arrived, but he did not go to Van Bristow's house. He did not announce his coming. He went by the less frequented streets of the near-by village to its inadequate hotel, where he found only a drummer for a New York shoe house and a gentleman traveling "out of Chicago" with samples of ready-made clothing.

For a time he sat in the dingy parlor of the place and listened to the jarring talk of the commercial travelers. Already Galavia and the months which had been, seemed receding into an improbable dream, but the misery of their bequeathing was poignantly real.

He rose impatiently and made his way to the livery-stable, where he hired a saddle horse. His idea was merely to be alone. The reins hung on the neck of his spiritless mount and the roads he went were the roads it took of its own unguided selection.

Suddenly Benton looked up. He was in a lane between overarching trees; a lane which he remembered. Off to the side were the hills bristling with pines, raised against the sky like the lances of marching troops. It was the road he had ridden with her on that day when her horse fell at the fence—

and there, on the side of the hill, stood a dilapidated cabin: the cabin upon whose porch he had poured water over her hands from a gourd dipper.

It was only the end of September, but an early frost had flushed the woods and hillsides into a hint of the crimson and gold they were soon to wear in more profligate splendor. The fragrant, blue mist of wood smoke drifted over the fields at the foot of the knobs. The hills were seen through a wash of purple. From somewhere to the far left drifted the mellowed music of fox-hounds. Riding slowly, the man came at length to the cabin gate.

The same farmer sat as indolently now as then, on the top step. The setter dog started up to growl as the horseman dismounted.

The man did not recognize him, but the proffer of Benton's cigar-case proved a sufficient credential, and a discussion of the weather appeared a satisfactory reason for remaining. It was only a verbal and logical step from weather to crops, and in ten minutes the visitor was being shown over the place. When the round of cribs and stables was completed it was time for the host to feed his stock, and, saying good-by at the barn, he left Benton to make his way alone to the cabin. Passing through the house from the back, the man halted suddenly and with abrupt wonderment at the front door.

For upright and slim, with a small gauntleted hand resting on one of the rude posts of the porch, gazing off intently into the coloring west, stood an unmistakable figure in a black riding habit. Incredulous, suddenly stunned under the cumulative suspense of the past three months, he stood hesitant. Then the figure slowly turned and, as the old heart-breaking, heart-recompensing smile came to her lips and eyes, the girl silently held out both arms to him.

Finally he found time to ask: "How long have you been here?"

"Six weeks," she answered. "And it's been lonesome."

"Your answer, Cara," he whispered. "What is your answer?"

"I am here," she said. "Don't you see me? I'm the answer."

THE END

BIOGRAPHIES

TWO POPULAR AUTHORS & SOMETHING ABOUT THEM

CHARLES NEVILLE BUCK

Though still a young man—he has only just passed his thirtieth year—Charles Neville Buck, the author of "The Lighted Match," has travelled far and done much. Although it was as late as January, 1909, that he first settled down to write for the magazines, he has made already an established reputation as a short story writer, and promises to make an even greater name as a novelist. His first novel, "The Key to Yesterday," was one of the successes of the last publishing season, and we shall be greatly surprised if "The Lighted Match" does not prove still more popular.

Born in Louisville, Ky., he visited South America with his father, the Hon. C. W. Buck, United States Minister to Peru. Since then he has travelled in Europe, covering the ground where he places the scenes in "The Key to Yesterday" and "The Lighted Match."

After graduation, Mr. Buck studied art, and for a year was the chief cartoonist on Louisville's leading daily paper. He then turned to editorial and reportorial work, which brought him into close contact with Kentucky politics and the mountain feuds. In 1902, while still a reporter, he was admitted to the Bar, but never practised.

Successful as he is at the short story, it is in the novel that Mr. Buck does his finest work. The novel rather than the short story gives scope for those little touches which make for style and atmosphere, and it is at these that Mr. Buck peculiarly excels. The vivid interest of his plots is apt to blind the reader to this merit, for Mr. Buck's novels have what some consider the only virtue of a novel, that they can be read for the story alone; but it is there, nevertheless, and for some constitutes the greatest charm of his work. In "The Lighted Match," even more than in "The Key to Yesterday," is this artistic finish noticeable. "The Lighted Match" is not only a bully good story, it is literature as well.

PELHAM GRANVILLE WODEHOUSE

During the past year a phrase has been frequently heard among magazine and book men in New York when the name of Pelham Granville Wodehouse has been mentioned. This phrase is "the logical successor to O. Henry"—and it is misleading. Any humorist who tried to follow in the tracks of O. Henry would be merely an imitator and the task would be as unwise as though O. Henry had cramped his own freedom in an effort to walk in the footprints of Mark Twain or any other predecessor in the field of humor.

Wodehouse suggests O. Henry only in that he has suddenly come into universal recognition as a remarkable humorist. He wields a pen which commands an uncommon power of satire, without the suggestion of vitriol or bitterness. His humor has a sparkle, effervescence and spontaneity which has put him in an incredibly short time in the front rank of writers, and since the materialistic barometer at least records the opinion of the editors and since the editors are supposed to know, has brought him into that envied coterie whose rate per word in the magazines has soared skyward.

P.G. Wodehouse was born in Guildford, England, in 1881, and while still an infant he accompanied his parents to Hong Kong, where the elder Wodehouse was a judge. He is a cousin of the Earl of Kimberley. In his school days he went in for cricket, football and boxing, and made for himself a reputation in athletics.

For two years Mr. Wodehouse went into a London bank and observed the passing parade from a high stool, but this was not quite in keeping with his tastes, and we find him next publishing a column of humorous paragraphs in the *London Globe*, under the head of "By the Way." Later he assumed the editorship of this department, and many of his paragraphs lived longer than the few hours' existence of most newspaper humor. Also since all writers experimentally venture into the dramatic, he wrote several vaudeville sketches which have had popular English productions.

Three years ago P.G. Wodehouse came to New York. He liked the American field and wanted to see whether his humor would strike the American fancy. It struck. Mr. Wodehouse had tried his wings here only a few months when magazine editors were bidding for his manuscripts. His short stories have appeared generally in the magazines, and while one often finds the delightful touch of pathos, there is always an abundance of laughter. In *Cosmopolitan, Collier's Weekly, Ainslee's*, and many other publications these stories appear as often as Mr. Wodehouse will contribute.

His novel, "The Intrusion of Jimmy," last year was a decided success. In it Mr. Wodehouse demonstrated his ability to hold his sprinting speed over a Marathon distance. The book, after giving the flattering returns of a large sale, found its second production on the stage. In its dramatized version with the title, "A Gentleman of Leisure," it has had its tryout on the road and has proven a success. With Douglas Fairbanks in the leading rôle, it will be one of next Fall's elaborate productions on Broadway.

In personality Mr. Wodehouse is quite as interesting as one might gather from his writings. Physically a man of splendid proportions and mentally a fountain of spirited humor, he is, nevertheless, modest to the point usually termed "retiring," and is well known only after long acquaintanceship. He is fond of all sports, and on reaching America became truly the native in his enthusiasm for baseball. Mr. Wodehouse says that one epoch of his literary career dates from his purchase of an automobile in 1907. The purchase was an investment of considerable gravity to a young writer just commencing to command an entree. The automobile lasted some two weeks and came to a violent end against a telephone pole. Mr. Wodehouse thought out the major problems of life sitting on the turf near the pole from a more or less lacerated point of view. He decided, among other things, that his *forte* was rather writing about motors than riding about *in* motors.

Mr. Wodehouse's second novel will be an even greater success than "The Intrusion of Jimmy." Mr. Wodehouse spent last winter on the Riviera writing this book, and his friends who have read the advance pages, agree with the publishers that it will deserve and receive even greater cordiality than the first. The title will be "The Prince and Betty," and it will be something for novel readers to look forward to.

CPSIA information can be obtained
at www.ICGtesting.com
Printed in the USA
LVHW041005020323
740706LV00008B/864